PRIVILEGE

DAG HEWARD-MILLS

Parchment House

Unless otherwise stated, all Scripture quotations are taken from the King James Version of the Bible.

THE PRIVILEGE

First published 2022 by Parchment House

Find out more about Dag Heward-Mills at:

Healing Jesus Campaign
Email: evangelist@daghewardmills.org
Website: www.daghewardmills.org
Facebook: Dag Heward-Mills
Twitter: @EvangelistDag

ISBN : 978-1-64330-273-7

Contents

CHAPTER 1

What is a Privilege?

For I testify that they gave as much as they were able, and even beyond their ability. Entirely on their own, THEY URGENTLY PLEADED WITH US FOR THE PRIVILEGE OF SHARING IN THIS SERVICE TO THE LORD'S PEOPLE.

2 Corinthians 8:3-4 (NIV)

Serving God's people will always be a privilege. There is no greater honour and no greater privilege than to become a servant of the Most High God. If you understand what it means to be a shepherd, you would plead for a chance to serve in that capacity.

A privilege is a special opportunity to do something. Actually, becoming a shepherd is a special opportunity given to you by God Himself.

A privilege is a right or benefit given to some people and not to others. Indeed, the benefits of being a shepherd are not enjoyed by everyone.

A privilege is a special advantage that is not enjoyed by everyone.

A privilege is a benefit enjoyed only by certain people.

A privilege is a special exemption granted to certain people.

A privilege is an advantage or source of pleasure granted to someone. God gives you an advantage and a source of blessings when He makes you a shepherd. Being a shepherd will be a blessing to you! Shepherds will care for people but the shepherd also receives many blessings because he is a shepherd.

The ministry of Jesus Christ is a privilege indeed. To be in the ministry is to be given a special opportunity to do something.

To become a shepherd is to be given a right and a benefit that is not given to others.

Not everyone enjoys the benefit of being a shepherd. Shepherds are given a special advantage that is not enjoyed by others.

You must grasp every opportunity that God gives you to be one of His shepherds.

The ministry of a shepherd is not a heavy load that changes your life negatively.

The ministry of Jesus Christ is not a burden. It is a privilege!

When God called you to be a shepherd, He was giving you a special advantage that is not experienced by many people.

It is important that you do not see God's call on your life as a bother. Do not see the work of a shepherd as an irritating inconvenience in your life!

God cannot inconvenience you! You must never show irritation on your face when it comes to the work of God. You must never complain when you are given a chance to be a shepherd. No one in his right mind will complain about a great privilege being given to him. It is only when you do not understand the privilege and the honour being done you that you would complain, murmur or grumble about being a shepherd.

This little book is an attempt to show you how privileged you are to be trained and appointed as a shepherd. From this time onwards, you must appreciate God's grace to you when invited to become a shepherd. Indeed, the grace of God that brings salvation has appeared to you! God is calling you to join the army of shepherds.

CHAPTER 2

The Privilege of Being a Shepherd Like Jesus

I am the good shepherd: the good shepherd giveth his life for the sheep.

John 10:11

A great privilege is bestowed upon you when you take up the job of a shepherd.

Jesus Christ was a shepherd! He called Himself the Good Shepherd!

If you accept to be a shepherd, you are actually accepting a privilege and not a job! You are privileged to have the job that Jesus Christ had on earth!

Jesus Christ was a shepherd. What an honour it is to join Jesus Christ Himself in His chosen profession!

The shepherding office is very important. That is why Jesus Himself did that job whilst He was on earth. Remember that sheep were scattered not because they didn't have an apostle or prophet, but because they didn't have a shepherd.

> **But when he saw the multitudes, he was moved with compassion on them, because they fainted, and were scattered abroad, as sheep having no shepherd.**
>
> **Matthew 9:36**

Jesus Christ called Himself the Good Shepherd. What a privilege to be able to join Jesus Christ, the Saviour of the world in this work of shepherding! A shepherd is a pastor and a covering for the sheep. The work of shepherding involves visiting people, praying for them, counselling with the word of God and interacting with them. The work of shepherding involves preaching and teaching the word of God. In Psalm 23, we have a clear picture of our Lord's shepherding activities. We are privileged to join Jesus Christ in these shepherding duties.

1. A shepherd is privileged to help people prosper.

"The Lord is my shepherd; I shall not want." (Psalm 23:1) "I shall not want" simply means I shall not be in difficulty, I shall not be poor and I shall not lack any good thing. A shepherd is privileged to help people to prosper.

2. **A shepherd is privileged to provide good food for the sheep.**

"He maketh me to lie down in green pastures." (Psalm 23:2). The best food for sheep is the green pasture. If you were a sheep, you would love it if your shepherd led you through green pastures. Jesus said to Peter, "If you love me, feed my sheep." (John 21:16).

The burden of owning animals is their dependence on you for food. If you run a zoo full of animals, you will discover how the animals depend on you for food. The dogs in your house are dependent on you for food. The horses in your stables are waiting for you to bring food to them. Every animal that you own depends on you for sustenance. That is why today there are hotels for dogs and cats so that the animals can be looked after while their owners are away. The sheep whom the Lord has given you are dependent on you for food. It is a privilege to feed God's people!

3. **A shepherd is privileged to lead people.**

"He leadeth me beside the still waters." (Psalm 23:2). Leadership is an important privilege of shepherds. Every shepherd is also a leader. Many people scramble to be leaders because of the privileges of being a leader. Indeed, it is a great privilege to be a leader.

Everything in a nation, in a church or a group rises and falls on the type of leaders there. In certain countries, you can literally see the countries come alive under the leadership of good leaders. Where there are bad leaders, the country is littered with huts, poor people and overflowing with criminals.

A good shepherd is a good leader! Every shepherd has the privilege of making himself into the best leader possible.

A shepherd must read books on leadership!

A shepherd must pass the tests of leadership!

A shepherd must avoid all the bad traits of poor leaders!

It is easy to find bad leaders! They are everywhere! Most poor countries are led by bad leaders! There are many countries that were once rich, prosperous and flourishing but have been made poor by bad leaders. It is interesting to observe the outcome of poor leadership. Leadership in the church is the same. Under a good shepherd, the church prospers and grows. Under bad leaders, the church goes around in circles.

Good leadership is not the same as being friendly. In cultures where friendship and relationships are important, people equate niceness with good leadership. Being handsome is not the same as being a good leader. Handsome people always attract a following. You will find out with time that being handsome or being a woman's man is not the same as being a good leader. As a shepherd you will have the privilege of being one of the good leaders of God's people.

4. A shepherd is privileged to restore the souls of people.

"He restoreth my soul." (Psalm 23:3). Every shepherd is a guide and a leader of fallen souls in need of salvation, cleansing, reconciliation, sanctification and holiness. The privilege of a shepherd is to restore people. The privilege of a shepherd is not to give up on anyone. "He restoreth my soul" speaks of the restorative power of a shepherd.

If you are a good shepherd, people will wonder how you are able to work with certain people. Those who are written off by others will become your jewels when you become a good shepherd. A good shepherd has the privilege of having people who look up to him with eyes of love - people who know that they would not exist without him. The Bible is clear: "… if any brother be overtaken in a fault, ye which are spiritual must restore such an one in the spirit of meekness, considering yourselves lest thou also be tempted." (Galatians 6:1).

5. **A shepherd is privileged to be with the people in the time of their difficulty.**

"Yea, though I walk through the valley of the shadow of death, I will fear no evil: for thou art with me; thy rod and thy staff they comfort me." (Psalm 23:4). A shepherd is privileged to be with people in their time of great crisis. He must be physically present at the scene of the trouble. This is why heads of state make an effort to appear at disaster zones when things happen. Presidents are criticized when they do not show up on the scene of tragedy, sorrow and death. In a sense, a president is like the shepherd of the whole nation. His presence alone calms things down.

A shepherd will attend more and more sad functions as the years go by.

A shepherd is expected to make himself available in the valley of the shadow of death. The valley of the shadow of death speaks of the dark places and difficult seasons of life.

A shepherd has the privilege of standing with the sheep in hospital.

A shepherd has the privilege of being in the home of bereaved ones.

A shepherd has the privilege of being at the funeral home.

A shepherd has the privilege of being at the graveside.

A shepherd has the privilege of wielding a rod and a staff to comfort the sheep.

6. **A shepherd is privileged to help the sheep overcome their enemies.**

"Thou preparest a table before me in the presence of mine enemies." (Psalm 23:5). A shepherd has the privilege of warding off the enemies of the sheep. Life is full of enemies. Everyone on this earth lives under a constant threat of enemies. Sometimes an enemy is far away but what he says, thinks or does affects you in your house. A shepherd has the privilege of stabilizing, encouraging and helping the sheep overcome their enemies.

Enemies are full of hatred.

Enemies wish they could destroy you.

Enemies wish they could consume you.

They are full of jealousy and hatred.

Oh, how your enemies wish to hear some bad news about you!

Through your privileged shepherding work, the sheep will overcome evil spirits, overcome evil men, overcome strange women and overcome satan himself. It is a privilege to fight the enemies of God's people.

7. A shepherd is privileged to anoint the sheep.

"...Thou anointest my head with oil; my cup runneth over." (Psalm 23:5). A shepherd is privileged to anoint the sheep. It is only by the power of the Holy Spirit that any Christian can become whom he is supposed to be. A shepherd is privileged to help people to receive the Holy Spirit through the power of God.

In the Middle East, shepherds rub their sheep with ointment to ward off the flies and insects. The smell of the ointment keeps the flies away from the sheep. It is your privilege to rub your sheep with ointment.

Anoint them with oil!

Reinhard Bonnke said the Lord told him to have Fire Conferences so that all the new converts at his crusades would receive the Holy Spirit and speak in tongues. This effort to let the new converts receive the Holy Spirit and speak in tongues is the shepherd anointing the sheep with oil. What a privilege to ensure that your sheep receive the Holy Spirit and speak in tongues.

CHAPTER 3

The Privilege of Being Honoured As a Shepherd

For every high priest taken from among men is ordained for men in things pertaining to God, that he may offer both gifts and sacrifices for sins: Who can have compassion on the ignorant, and on them that are out of the way; for that he himself also is compassed with infirmity. And by reason hereof he ought, as for the people, so also for himself, to offer for sins. And NO MAN TAKETH THIS HONOUR UNTO HIMSELF, but he that is called of God, as was Aaron.

Hebrews 5:1-4

A great honour is bestowed upon you when you take up the job of a shepherd.

Jesus Christ was an honoured shepherd! He called Himself the Good Shepherd!

If you accept to be a shepherd, you are actually accepting an honour and not a job! You are privileged and honoured by Jesus Christ!

Jesus Christ was a shepherd. What an honour it is to join Jesus Christ Himself in His profession!

No one takes this honour to himself. Which honour is this? The honour of being a priest and an intercessor for God's people!

What a privilege it is to have been honoured by God. When you become a shepherd, you have received honour from God Himself. Honour is something that is bestowed on you. You cannot honour yourself. Every country has a way of honouring its citizens. In England, the Queen bestows honour on those she deems worthy. People receive Nobel prizes as signs of honour for their achievements in various fields of endeavour.

What is this honour for? Why is the job of shepherding an honour?

1. It is a great honour to be chosen from among men.

It is an honour to be chosen out of the group. Every shepherd is chosen from among men. On the day that you are chosen, there are several other people who could also be chosen. God chooses you out of a group and honours you above your colleagues. It is indeed a great privilege.

2. It is a great honour to be ordained to have a job in things pertaining to God.

Those who work in the banks have a job in things pertaining to dollars, pounds, shillings and cedis. Those who work in hospitals have a job in things pertaining to the human body, blood, sickness and disease. Those who work in construction have a job in things pertaining to cement, wood, nails, salaries of staff, etc. When you are a shepherd, you have a job in things pertaining to God.

3. **It is a great honour to relate to God directly on behalf of people.**

Those who work as shepherds spend their time offering gifts and sacrifices to God. This means they come in contact with God all the time. What an honourable job when you are constantly interacting with Almighty God on behalf of people. It is an honour to know about the gifts and sacrifices that people are making to their God.

These are private things that you are privileged to know about. What an honourable job this is, to relate directly with God. It is a privilege to be a go-between between the people and God.

4. **It is an honour to be chosen to have compassion on people.**

A person who is chosen to be a shepherd is expected to have compassion on the ignorant.

What an amazing job this is! God gives you the discretion to care for people in the best way you can.

Imagine that your job is to show mercy and kindness to people who need it! Is it not God who shows mercy to people? Are you not being given a job where you have to act like God and show kindness to people? What an honourable and highly esteemed position God is giving to you!

5. **It is an honour to be chosen because you are surrounded with your own sins.**

> **And when Peter saw it, he answered unto the people, ye men of Israel, why marvel ye at this? or why look ye so earnestly on us, as though by our own power or holiness we had made this man to walk?**
>
> **Acts 3:12**

If you were qualified to do the job of a shepherd, perhaps, it would be different. But you clearly do not qualify. You are yourself compassed about with sin and iniquity. What a privilege therefore it is to find a place in the leadership of the church! Peter knew that he was not a shepherd because he was a holy man.

CHAPTER 4

The Privilege of Being Brought Near As a Shepherd

And Moses said unto Korah, Hear, I pray you, ye sons of Levi: SEEMETH IT BUT A SMALL THING UNTO YOU, that the God of Israel hath separated you from the congregation of Israel, TO BRING YOU NEAR TO HIMSELF to do the service of the tabernacle of the Lord, and to stand before the congregation to minister unto them? And HE HATH BROUGHT THEE NEAR TO HIM, and all thy brethren the sons of Levi with thee: and seek ye the priesthood also? For which cause both thou and all thy company are gathered together against the Lord: and what is Aaron, that ye murmur against him?

Numbers 16:8-11

You are being brought near when you take up the job of a shepherd.

Jesus Christ was a great shepherd! He called Himself the Good Shepherd!

If you accept to be a shepherd, you are actually just being brought near! Being a shepherd is being brought near to Jesus Christ and to God!

Jesus Christ was a shepherd. What an honour it is to be drawn closer and closer still!

1. It is a privilege to be made a shepherd of God's people:

Korah was privileged to be a leader in the house of God. Korah and certain sons of Levi were filled with pride and forgot about the great privilege that had been shown to them in making them shepherds. Moses pointed out the greatness of the shepherding job to these proud upstarts.

2. It is a privilege to be separated from the congregation:

Korah was privileged to be separated from the rest of the congregation. God indeed separated you from the rest of the masses when He decided to make you a shepherd. It is a great privilege to be separated from the rest of the congregation for the great and honourable job of being a shepherd.

3. It is a privilege to be brought near to God.

Korah was privileged to be brought near because of his appointment to leadership. When you become a shepherd, you are automatically brought near to God. If you are made a minister of state, you are automatically brought near to the president of the nation. My job as a shepherd has not brought me near to surgeons and physicians. It has brought me near to God. Today, you must relish the blessing of being brought near. It is an honour to be brought near to see, to hear and to know things that few will ever know.

Nearness is the great privilege that must be cherished and guarded fiercely. Your "near" relationship with God is what gives birth to everything else. Your "near" relationship with anyone is what yields amazing fruits. Whenever you have a chance to choose, choose nearness rather than money. There are people who take certain jobs because they will earn more money. It is better to be near with a lower salary than to be far away with a higher salary.

Almighty God was angry with Korah because he did not value his nearness to God.

4. It is a privilege for your family to be brought near as well.

Korah's family was privileged to be brought near. The ministry is a privilege because your family gets to be brought closer as well. Korah forgot all the privileges that he had and began to accuse Moses of wrongdoing.

CHAPTER 5

The Privilege of Joining a Special Family of Shepherds

Then the Lord spoke to Moses, saying, "BRING THE TRIBE OF LEVI NEAR AND SET THEM BEFORE AARON THE PRIEST, THAT THEY MAY SERVE HIM. And they shall perform the duties for him and for the whole congregation before the tent of meeting, to do the service of the tabernacle. They shall also keep all the furnishings of the tent of meeting, along with the duties of the sons of Israel, to do the service of the tabernacle. YOU SHALL THUS GIVE THE LEVITES TO AARON AND TO HIS SONS; THEY ARE WHOLLY GIVEN TO HIM FROM AMONG THE SONS OF ISRAEL. So you shall appoint Aaron and his sons that they may keep their priesthood, but the layman who comes near shall be put to death." Again the Lord spoke to Moses, saying, "Now, behold, I HAVE TAKEN THE LEVITES FROM AMONG THE SONS OF ISRAEL instead of every first-born, the first issue of the womb among the sons of Israel. So the Levites shall be Mine.

Numbers 3:5-12 (NASB)

If you accept to be a shepherd, you are actually accepting to be a part of a special family of shepherds!

A great privilege is bestowed upon you when you take up the job of a shepherd.

Jesus Christ is the good shepherd! He called Himself the Good Shepherd!

You are privileged to join a unique family!

Jesus Christ was a shepherd. What a privilege it is to join this family where Jesus Christ Himself is the head!

1. It is a privilege to be a part of the tribe of Levi.

When you become a shepherd, you join a special family – the family of Levi.

One of the greatest privileges of being a shepherd is that you are part of a special family. A family of shepherds! A family of priests!

When you become a shepherd, you join the brotherhood of priests. As part of the Levitical family, you enjoy all the privileges and benefits of the Levites. When God welcomes you into the work of a shepherd, you have been privileged to be part of this amazing family.

Today, all my close spiritual brothers and sisters are "Levites". Almost every friend that I have is a pastor. Almost every close relative that I have is a pastor or a shepherd. My entire social life revolves in and around the lives of other shepherds and pastors.

2. It is a privilege to live for God and not for money.

"Bring the tribe of Levi near and set them before Aaron the priest, that they may serve him" (Numbers 3:6 (NASB)). Not everyone serves God! Many people serve their bellies! Most people serve money! It is a privilege to have been chosen to serve something higher and greater than money.

Remember that the earth is cursed because of the sins of Adam. Because the ground yields very little, it is very difficult to prosper. It is very difficult to prosper and most men live their lives trying to get something to eat or drink. God has given you the privilege of being a shepherd. Your life will therefore be spent serving God instead of following after money. As a shepherd, you have the privilege of having a higher kind of life. As a shepherd, God has given you the rare privilege of being a Levite.

3. It is a privilege to be chosen to work in the tabernacle.

Working in the tabernacle is like working in God's bedroom. To be invited to work in someone's bedroom, you must be very close and personal. God has His personal servants who come to work on the furnishings of the tabernacle. They have duties in the innermost sanctum. Their lives and duties have to do with the personal things of God.

What a privilege to be asked to work in the private and sanctified space where God has chosen to work among men! What a privilege to be a shepherd! If God has given you a chance to be a shepherd do not joke with it! If God has given you a chance to be a shepherd do not hide from Him!

CHAPTER 6

The Privilege of a High-Ranking Job Like Shepherding

Brethren, I count not myself to have apprehended: but this one thing I do, forgetting those things which are behind, and reaching forth unto those things which are before, I press toward the mark for the prize of THE HIGH CALLING OF GOD IN CHRIST JESUS. Let us therefore, as many as be perfect, be thus minded: and if in any thing ye be otherwise minded, God shall reveal even this unto you. Nevertheless, whereto we have already attained, let us walk by the same rule, let us mind the same thing. Brethren, be followers together of me, and mark them which walk so as ye have us for an ensample.

Philippians 3:13-17

A great privilege is bestowed upon you when you take up the high-ranking job of a shepherd.

Jesus Christ is the Good Shepherd! He called Himself the Good Shepherd!

If you accept to be a shepherd, you are actually accepting a high-ranking job.

You are privileged to have a high-ranking job.

Jesus Christ was a shepherd. What a privilege it is to have a high-ranking job!

Why Shepherding is a High-Ranking Job

1. **A shepherd's job is high-ranking because God Himself does that job.**

> Shepherd the flock of God among you, exercising oversight not under compulsion, but voluntarily, according to the will of God; and not for sordid gain, but with eagerness;
>
> 1 Peter 5:2 (NASB)

2. **A shepherd's job is considered to be high-ranking because Jesus Christ Himself does that job.**

> Now the God of peace, that brought again from the dead our Lord Jesus, that great shepherd of the sheep, through the blood of the everlasting covenant,
>
> Hebrews 13:20

3. **A shepherd's job is considered to be a high-ranking job because it is a high calling.**

> I press toward the mark for the prize of the high calling of God in Christ Jesus.
>
> Philippians 3:14

The call to be a shepherd is a high calling. It is a high calling because that is the call Jesus had – the call to be a shepherd. The privilege of a high calling must not be taken lightly. The high calling of God is a call to an important job. The high calling of God is a call to a superior position.

Perhaps, in this life you will never have a more important job than to be a shepherd. Being a shepherd is a distinguished and exalted position. If you are a shepherd, God has given you a big-time job in His house.

Remember that all of us are the sheep of His hand. God Himself is our Shepherd. God is elevating you from being one of the sheep to being one of the shepherds. This is what Paul calls the high calling of God in Christ Jesus.

4. Being a shepherd is high-ranking because you are a manager in God's house.

> And when all the land of Egypt was famished, the people cried to Pharaoh for bread: and Pharaoh said unto all the Egyptians, Go unto Joseph; what he saith to you, do.
>
> Genesis 41:55

You are the person who has control and direction of the institution. The direction in which everything will go depends on you. You are the one who handles and controls the resources of the church. If the church prospers, it is up to you. If the church is impoverished it is also your fault.

5. Being a shepherd is high-ranking because you are a supervisor in God's house.

Is it not a blessing to be made a supervisor?

> And Joseph found grace in his sight, and he served him: and he made him OVERSEER OVER HIS HOUSE, and all that he had he put into his hand. And it came to pass from the time that he had made him OVERSEER in his house, AND OVER ALL THAT HE HAD, that the Lord blessed the Egyptian's house for Joseph's sake; and the

> blessing of the Lord was upon all that he had in the house, and in the field.
>
> Genesis 39:4-5

6. **Being a shepherd is high-ranking because you are a director in God's house.**

> But made his own people to go forth like sheep, and guided them in the wilderness like a flock. And he led them on safely, so that they feared not: but the sea overwhelmed their enemies.
>
> Psalm 78:52-53

Is it not a privilege for God to raise you up to become a director in His house? In many ways, a shepherd directs the lives of the sheep. What an honour and a privilege!

7. **Being a shepherd is high-ranking because you are an administrator in God's house.**

> So Potiphar gave Joseph complete administrative responsibility over everything he owned. With Joseph there, he didn't worry about a thing—except what kind of food to eat! Joseph was a very handsome and well-built young man,
>
> Genesis 39:6 (NLT)

What a privilege for you to administer God's wisdom, power and gifts to His people. He has made you like Joseph who was the administrator of Egypt. The problem of hunger was solved by Joseph. Joseph administered all the grain and all the food and all the provisions to the people of Egypt. This will be your job as a shepherd – to remove hunger, want and need.

8. **Being a shepherd is high-ranking because you are a governor in God's house.**

During the colonial era, Great Britain appointed governors over their colonies. There was a governor in Nigeria, a governor in Ghana, a governor in Sierra Leone. One of the famous governors in Ghana was called Sir Gordon Guggisberg. Gordon Guggisberg proposed a ten-year development plan and also sixteen principles of education for Ghana. He built the school I attended, the Achimota School, the deep water Takoradi Harbour and increased the length of the motorable roads in the country. He also built the famous Korle-bu Teaching Hospital where I was trained to be a doctor. These governors were basically Prime Ministers of the countries. They had plans to develop the countries and educate their colonies.

If God has made you a governor of His church, He is expecting you to develop the church and to educate the members of the church. What a great honour it is for God to make you a governor!

Can't you see that you have been given a high-ranking job? You must develop the church and educate the members with the word of God.

9. **Being a shepherd is high-ranking because you are a superintendent and an overseer in God's house.**

> And Joseph found grace in his sight, and he served him: and he made him OVERSEER OVER HIS HOUSE, and all that he had he put into his hand. And it came to pass from the time that he had made him OVERSEER in his house, AND OVER ALL THAT HE HAD, that the LORD blessed the Egyptian's house for Joseph's sake; and the blessing of the LORD was upon all that he had in the house, and in the field.
>
> Genesis 39:4-5

Notice how Joseph was described as the overseer of the house of Potiphar. A shepherd oversees everything. Just like Joseph in Egypt, everything is put into the hands of the overseer. God is making you the overseer of all of God's people. What a privilege that is! A shepherd is truly the superintendent and overseer of the house of God.

10. Being a shepherd is high-ranking because you are delivered from all low-ranking, routine and minor jobs.

> And the Lord said unto Moses, Gather unto me seventy men of the elders of Israel, WHOM THOU KNOWEST TO BE THE ELDERS OF THE PEOPLE, AND OFFICERS OVER THEM; and bring them unto the tabernacle of the congregation, that they may stand there with thee. And I will come down and talk with thee there: and I will take of the spirit which is upon thee, and will put it upon them; and they shall bear the burden of the people with thee, that thou bear it not thyself alone.
>
> Numbers 11:16-17

Being a shepherd is to be elevated above the rank of a subordinate for the rest of your life. Even if you are given an inferior and sub-standard job in the secular world, in the house of God you are elevated into the distinguished and exceptional position of a shepherd. You will never be called second-rate in the house of God. There is nothing dull or inferior about the job of a shepherd - you will notice that the people who were chosen to bear the burden with Moses were elders and officers in the congregation.

CHAPTER 7

The Privilege of Being Part of a Government of Shepherds

And God hath set some in the church, first apostles, secondarily prophets, thirdly teachers, after that miracles, then gifts of healings, helps, GOVERNMENTS, diversities of tongues.

1 Corinthians 12:28

A great privilege is bestowed upon you when you take up the job of a shepherd.

Jesus Christ is the Good Shepherd and shepherds govern the church of God.

If you accept to be a shepherd, you are actually accepting to be a part of the government of the church.

Even if you are not a part of the government of your country, you are privileged to be a part of the government of the church!

Jesus Christ was a shepherd. What a privilege it is to be a part of God's government!

The privilege of being a shepherd is that you are offered an invitation to be a part of a government. God has given you the privilege of being part of governing His church.

Shepherding is an opportunity to use the gift of governments. What a privilege it is to be a part of a government! What is the gift of government? The word "government" is translated from the Greek word, *kubernesis,* which means a steering, pilotage, or guiding. This gift of governments is exactly the same thing as the gift of being a shepherd or pastor.

The shepherd is to use the gift of governments to guide the sheep to "good places" (green pastures - Psalm 23:2).

Many people live their whole lives trying to get into government. They desire to be in places of authority and have the job and the privilege of being in the government. They would love to be the president, the vice president or a minister of state. After each election people are heartbroken and disappointed because they did not win. I have seen many people disillusioned and lifeless when they are not chosen to be part of the government. Being part of a government is truly a privileged job. But it is a privilege that God is inviting you to. God is giving you the privilege of being a part of the government of His church.

We need to soberly reflect on the implications of leading people. When someone does not have the ability to govern in the natural, the whole nation is thrown into chaos. There are bad governments everywhere. The level of poverty, war, and instability that exist in many countries reveals the lack of good governments. When God invites you to be a shepherd, He is inviting you to be at the very top of society.

CHAPTER 8

The Privilege of Having a Job That Requires Very High Qualifications of a Shepherd

A bishop then must be blameless, the husband of one wife, vigilant, sober, of good behaviour, given to hospitality, apt to teach; Not given to wine, no striker, not greedy of filthy lucre; but patient, not a brawler, not covetous; One that ruleth well his own house, having his children in subjection with all gravity; (For if a man know not how to rule his own house, how shall he take care of the church of God?) Not a novice, lest being lifted up with pride he fall into the condemnation of the devil. Moreover he must have a good report of them which are without; lest he fall into reproach and the snare of the devil.

1 Timothy 3:2-7

A great privilege is bestowed upon you when you take up the job of a shepherd.

Jesus Christ is the Good Shepherd! He called Himself the Good Shepherd!

If you are accepted as a shepherd, it actually proves that you have very high qualifications.

Jesus Christ had very high qualifications. What a privilege it is to join this family where only those with very high qualifications are a part!

The privilege of becoming a shepherd is that it is an offer and an invitation to have a job that requires you to be highly qualified.

There are few jobs that require as high a qualification as shepherding.

1. To become a shepherd, you must have a desire for the privilege of shepherding.

I have never heard of a job in the bank for which you must first have a desire.

It is a good thing for church members to desire the work of a bishop. As you are filled with a desire for God's work, a great grace will come over you. People in the church must be taught to aspire for the highest positions in the church. It is biblical to desire the highest office in the church.

> **This is a true saying, If a man desire the office of a bishop, he desireth a good work.**
>
> **1 Timothy 3:1**

Do not just desire to be an usher! Do not just desire to sing in the choir! Desire to be a shepherd! I used to play the drums and the organ in church. But I wanted to go as high as I could. I wanted to be a shepherd!

2. **To become a privileged shepherd, you must have a divine call.**

You must have a divine call. The ministry is not a human institution. The Bible makes it clear that you need to have a divine call to serve in a certain capacity.

> **And no man taketh this honour unto himself, but he that is CALLED OF GOD, as was Aaron.**
>
> **Hebrews 5:4**

One of the manifestations of a divine call is a supernatural desire and interest in the work of the ministry. Paul had a supernatural interest for the salvation of all men, including the Jews.

> **Brethren, my heart's desire and prayer to God for Israel is, that they might be saved.**
>
> **Romans 10:1**

Paul had this desire in him and it was this desire that was translated into practical ministry time and time again. Do not take the call of God lightly. You could pay with your life for disobeying the divine call.

I want to emphasize here that it is important to respond to the call of God on your life. If you were standing downstairs and your boss called for you from upstairs, wouldn't you run to him? What do you think would happen if you ignored his calls when he knew that you could hear him? You might lose your job! If God calls you and you refuse to heed the call, you might be endangering your very life. Accept the privilege right now and flow with the call of God!

3. **You must be willing to be a shepherd.**

> **...for necessity is laid upon me; yea, woe is unto me, if I preach not the gospel! FOR IF I DO THIS THING**

WILLINGLY, I have a reward: but if against my will, a dispensation of the gospel is committed unto me.

1 Corinthians 9:16-17

There must be a willing commitment to obey the call of God on your life. Some people know that they are called! They even have a desire to do the work, yet you do not see any commitment in them.

Notice that Isaiah didn't say, "Here am I, SEND HIM!" He said, "Here am I, send ME!" (Isaiah 6:8). To offer yourself, is a sign that you are willing.

Make great efforts to be available and involved in day-to-day church life. If there is no extra commitment or willing sacrifice you are missing something.

4. You must have a godly character.

A bishop then must be blameless, the husband of one wife, vigilant, sober, of good behaviour, given to hospitality, apt to teach; Not given to wine, no striker, not greedy of filthy lucre; but patient, not a brawler, not covetous; One that ruleth well his own house, having his children in subjection with all gravity; (For if a man know not how to rule his own house, how shall he take care of the church of God?) Not a novice, lest being lifted up with pride he fall into the condemnation of the devil.

1 Timothy 3:2-6

There is no substitute for godliness and a good character. Your faithfulness is the cornerstone of your character. When I started out in ministry, I was impressed by well-spoken people. As the years passed, I lost confidence in the outward presentation. I have found people who are quiet, not so impressive, but faithful in character. These people are to be preferred one hundred times more than outwardly impressive pastors. Your Bible school certificate, your nice dressing and ability to sing will not earn you a position in the pastorate. It is a great privilege for you to be selected for this honour.

Even with stringent character filters, we still have some sticks turning out to be snakes. Whenever there is a test, you will notice some of your firewood sticks turn into snakes. Remember the incident when Paul was gathering some sticks to light a fire. When he lit the fire, a snake jumped out from among the sticks. (Acts 28:3).

As a senior pastor, beware of people whom you feel under pressure to promote. Beware of people whom you feel under pressure to show appreciation to. Beware of people whom you feel under pressure to increase their salaries. Such people will not be satisfied with any show of love. There is only one qualification for people who want to join the pastoral team - they have to stay around long enough. They have to "company" around long enough for time and the elements to test them.

Pastors, do not just accept impressive ministers from other churches to work with you. It could be the mistake of your life. When the apostles had to choose a replacement for Judas, what did they say? Whom did they choose?

> **Wherefore of these men which have COMPANIED WITH US all the time that the Lord Jesus went in and out among us, Beginning from the baptism of John, unto that same day that he was taken up from us, must one be ordained to be a witness with us of his resurrection.**
>
> **Acts 1:21-22**

What did they do? They didn't choose the best worship leader or the most charismatic speaker. I take no notice of sweet words showered on me by some job-seekers. All I say in my mind is, "I commend you to God and to time."

No one can be a shepherd unless you know his character. You can never know someone's character unless you have known him for some years.

The whole of 1 Timothy 3 is a catalogue of character qualifications for every serious-minded minister. Read it for yourselves. You will not read anything about a bishop or pastor having to be anointed or gifted. There is no instruction that a pastor must be talented or charming.

5. **To become a shepherd, your wife must also have some qualifications.**

The character of the pastor's wife has a bearing on his ministry (1 Timothy 3:11). A Bible school certificate is not the only qualification for the ministry.

6. **To become a shepherd, you must be blameless.**

To become a shepherd, you must be sober, vigilant, of good behaviour, apt to teach, not given to wine, not quarrelsome and not greedy for money (1 Timothy 3:2-3, 8).

7. **To become a shepherd you must be patient, a ruler of your own house, not a novice, of good report and already proved and tested.**

> **...but patient, not a brawler, not covetous; One that ruleth well his own house, having his children in subjection with all gravity;**
> **Not a novice, lest being lifted up with pride he fall into the condemnation of the devil. Moreover he must have a good report of them which are without; ...**
>
> **1 Timothy 3:3-4, 6-7**

CHAPTER 9

The Privilege of Becoming a Highly Skilled Shepherd

I am the good shepherd, and know my sheep, and am known of mine.

John 10 : 14

Jesus Christ is the highly skilled Great Shepherd! He called Himself the Good Shepherd!

A great privilege is bestowed upon you when you take up the job of a shepherd because you will become highly skilled too.

If you accept to be a shepherd, you are actually accepting to be a part of a special family of highly skilled men!

You are privileged to join a family with a unique set of special skills.

What a privilege it is to join this family of highly skilled shepherds.

The privilege of being a shepherd is that it is an offer and an invitation to become a highly skilled person. You will have to develop several skills if you are going to become a shepherd. Apart from meeting the requirements, you need to develop certain skills.

Unskilled people are usually the poorest in the world. For instance, people who harvest pepper and tomatoes are much poorer than those who make and sell iPhones and cars. It takes much more skill to make an iPhone or a car than it does to harvest pepper and oranges. Generally, the more skills you have the richer you become.

Becoming a shepherd allows you to develop a set of skills that are so valuable that they make you into a prosperous person. Are you not honoured to develop a set of skills that turn you into a prosperous person?

Anyone who is unskilled in this life is doomed to poverty. There must be something that you are able to do well. Can you type? Can you play an instrument? Can you drive a car? Can you use software? Can you win a case in court? Can you look after sick people? Can you turn cocoa into chocolate? Can you turn oranges into orange juice? All these are skills that make people rich. Without any skill, no one will need you or want you.

Let us go through some of the skills that are needed to be a shepherd.

Special Skills of a Shepherd

1. The skill of relating with God

It is a privilege to relate with God! Relating with God is a skill you must learn. Most people do not know how to relate with God. A disciplined person who has consistent prayer and personal Bible study shows a deep relationship with God. Without a personal relationship with God, you are going nowhere.

2. The skill of listening to preaching videos

Your ability to listen to preaching and teaching videos for long hours shows that you will one day be a preacher. It is a skill that many people do not have.

3. The skill of watching pastors/people preaching

You will become what you are watching all the time. Your ability to watch preaching and teaching for long hours reveals how you will be preaching yourself one day. It is a skill which many people do not have.

4. The skill of waiting on God

To wait on God in a room or a house for days on end is a skill that few people have. If you do not wait on God, you will not hear from Him. They that wait upon the Lord shall renew their strength (Isaiah 40:31). In the book of Acts, Apostle Paul was waiting on God with some prophets and teachers. As they waited on God and ministered to him, the Holy Spirit spoke and began a brand-new mission to the ends of the world. This new and amazing mission would never have come to pass if they had not learnt how to wait on the Lord.

Now there were in the church that was at Antioch certain prophets and teachers; as Barnabas, and

Simeon that was called Niger, and Lucius of Cyrene, and Manaen, which had been brought up with Herod the tetrarch, and Saul. As they ministered to the Lord, and fasted, the Holy Ghost said, Separate me Barnabas and Saul for the work whereunto I have called them. And when they had fasted and prayed, and laid their hands on them, they sent them away.

Acts 13:1-3

5. People-handling skills

The phrase "apt to teach" (1 Timothy 3:2) reveals the ability of a shepherd to lead and influence people. Teaching includes being able to handle people of all sorts. A person who is quarrelsome and cantankerous will not have people handling skills. Shepherding is a great privilege because you will learn people handling skills. Once you know how to handle people you are ready to be a great leader.

6. Leadership skills

So the Lord said to Moses, "Take Joshua son of Nun, a man IN WHOM IS THE SPIRIT OF LEADERSHIP, and lay your hand on him."

Numbers 27:18 (NIV)

Leadership is a skill which is developed in every shepherd. This is because a shepherd is basically a leader. The art of leadership is much more than meets the eye. Most people who are in leadership are natural leaders and they do what comes to them naturally. Everyone who is trained in shepherding will be trained in leadership skills. What a privilege it is to have such life skills!

7. Preaching skills

People who want to be shepherds or lay pastors must develop the ability to teach and to preach. The principal duty of a shepherd is to feed the flocks. Someone who wants to be a shepherd must demonstrate experience in preaching and teaching. The best way to learn how to preach is to listen to preaching tapes and preach the same thing. Timothy was told to preach the same things that he had heard Paul preaching.

> **And the things that thou hast heard of me among many witnesses, THE SAME commit thou to faithful men...**
>
> **2 Timothy 2:2**

CHAPTER 10

The Privilege of Royalty

But watch thou in all things, endure afflictions, do the work of an evangelist, make full proof of thy ministry. For I am now ready to be offered, and the time of my departure is at hand. I have fought a good fight, I have finished my course, I have kept the faith: Henceforth THERE IS LAID UP FOR ME A CROWN OF RIGHTEOUSNESS, which the Lord, the righteous judge, shall give me at that day: and not to me only, but unto all them also that love his appearing.

2 Timothy 4:5-8

A great privilege is bestowed upon you when you take up the job of a shepherd.

Jesus Christ is the King of kings and the Lord of lords! If you accept to be a shepherd, you are actually accepting to be a part of the royal family of heaven.

You are privileged to join a royal family! In heaven, you will not be outside the royal family and looking in.

Jesus Christ is a shepherd and a king! When you become a shepherd, you will also become a shepherd and a king. What a privilege it is to join the royal family where Jesus Christ Himself will be the King of kings and the Lord of lords!

By doing the work of a shepherd, you are most likely to inherit a crown of life, a crown of righteousness and a crown of glory. Remember that a crown is given to only those who are royalty. Apart from the Queen of England, and other royalty, few other people wear crowns on earth.

Imagine that you are going to be part of the royal family when you get to heaven. Those of us who could not be part of a royal family on earth and who could never enter a palace to see what was behind the walls, will have a chance to experience royalty at its best.

Three different crowns are promised. A crown of life, a crown of righteousness and a crown of glory! What will you be doing wearing a crown if you are not part of a royal family? The crown of life is promised in two different passages of the Bible. However, the crown of glory and the crown of righteousness are promised in one passage.

> **Blessed is the man that endureth temptation: for when he is tried, HE SHALL RECEIVE THE CROWN OF LIFE, which the Lord hath promised to them that love him.**
>
> **James 1:12**

And unto the angel of the church in Smyrna write; These things saith the first and the last, which was dead, and is alive; I know thy works, and tribulation, and poverty, (but thou art rich) and I know the blasphemy of them which say they are Jews, and are not, but are of the synagogue of Satan.
Fear none of those things which thou shalt suffer: behold, the devil shall cast some of you into prison, that ye may be tried; and ye shall have tribulation ten days: be thou faithful unto death, and I will give thee A CROWN OF LIFE.

Revelation 2:8-10

The elders which are among you I exhort, who am also an elder, and a witness of the sufferings of Christ, and also a partaker of the glory that shall be revealed: feed the flock of God which is among you, taking the oversight thereof, not by constraint, but willingly; not for filthy lucre, but of a ready mind; Neither as being lords over God's heritage, but being ensamples to the flock.
And when the chief Shepherd shall appear, ye shall receive a CROWN OF GLORY that fadeth not away.

1 Peter 5:1-4

Imagine that! Three whole crowns waiting for you! You will soon be even more glorious than the king or queen of England! And all this, just because you were a shepherd!

As part of the royal family in heaven, you will have many new privileges and blessings.

Blessings of becoming Royalty in Heaven

1. You will have the honour of wearing a crown.
2. You will have the honour of staying in a palace.
3. You will have the honour of wearing jewels.

4. You will have the honour having many servants.
5. You will have the honour of wearing beautiful royal clothes.
6. You will have the honour of relating with other members of the royal family in heaven.
7. You will have the honour of having special food made for you.
8. You will have the honour learning the king's protocol.
9. You will be closer to the throne and closer to where the action is.
10. You will have the honour of going for royal tours and royal holidays.
11. You will have the honour of greeting the public with a royal wave.
12. You will be honoured and celebrated as royalty throughout eternity.

Conclusion

It is time to take up the privilege of shepherding. God has His eyes on you and that is why He is giving you this special privilege. Forget those things that are behind. Many sad and bad things have already happened. They are such that you cannot undo them. You cannot unwind! You cannot change them! There are many things like that in this world. The only way to overcome them is to forget them. Thinking about them takes you deeper and further into despair and despondency. Only God can heal certain things! It is time for you to forget about the past so that you can reach out and be the shepherd that God wants you to be.

Reach forward to the privileges that are before you. God has called you to do great things for Him. You must reach forward to the mark of the high calling. You will not attain to the high calling by sitting in one position.

You must reach forth to the privileges that seem to be out of range. It is only by reaching forth to new things that you will forget the past and bear fruit. If you are following the Holy Spirit, you are not likely to be at the same spot in a year's time. The Spirit is always moving and as you follow Him, the main characteristic of your life will be movement. I see God changing things and shifting things around!

Walruses can deliberately push their eyes out of their sockets so they can see sideways.

Walruses can kill intruding seals by hugging them to death.

The Latin name for a walrus is *Odobenus rosmarus*, which literally means 'tooth-walking seahorse.'

Sheep

Scientists have found that sheep can recognise the faces of other sheep.

If you leave sheep to wander around a maze, they tend to turn left.

China has blue sheep. The **bharal** can be found high up in the Himalayan mountains, where its grey coat with a bluish hue keeps it warm in the freezing temperatures.

In 2015, a Singapore Airlines freight plane was forced to make an emergency landing when the smoke alarm was set off by farting sheep.

In 1889, Alexander Graham Bell (the scientist who is credited with inventing the telephone) tried to create sheep with twice the normal number of nipples. He thought animals with extra nipples would produce extra milk. However, after years of trying and no success, he finally gave up in 1904.

Sloths

Sloths are famously slow – they move at about 3 metres a minute. Luckily, they can also spin their heads 270 degrees to watch out for any predators sneaking up on them.

Sloths move so slowly and stay still for so long that algae grows on their coat, giving them a green appearance and making them look as if they're wearing green clothes. They use it as camouflage to hide from predators, and can also eat the algae as a snack.

All mammals that live in trees poop from the branches – except sloths, who prefer to climb down to the ground to

release their waste there. This is a big risk, as most predators are on the ground. Fortunately they only have to do this every 4 to 8 days.

Sloths can have hundreds of insects living in their fur at any given time – mosquitoes, sandflies, lice, ticks, beetles, mites and moths all like to make a sloth their home. (Just one of many reasons why stroking a sloth is a really bad idea.)

Squirrels

Have you ever seen a human using a 'wingsuit'? We copied this idea from the flying squirrel. There are 50 different species of 'flying squirrel', which use furry flaps of skin running from their wrist to their ankle to glide through the air as far as 90 metres to the next tree.

California ground squirrels chew old rattlesnake skins and then lick themselves and pups – this makes them smell like a snake, and the real snakes leave them alone.

Squirrels plant a lot more trees than humans do. In 1998, scientists discovered that squirrels forget where they put 74 per cent of all the nuts they hide. Many of these nuts are buried in the ground, and grow into trees.

Tigers

The average tiger has over 100 stripes on its body, and just like human fingerprints, the stripe pattern is unique to each tiger.

A tiger's stripes aren't just in its fur, they're marked on its skin as well – so if you shaved a tiger (and good luck trying that), you'd still see its distinctive stripe pattern.

The first person to be killed by a tiger in Britain was a barmaid in a Wiltshire pub called the White Lion. In 1703, Hannah Twynnoy worked in

the pub which had live wild animals on display for entertainment, and it all went terribly wrong.

Whales

The biggest animal living on the planet is the blue whale, which is as loud as it is large – it can call underwater at a volume of 188 decibels, which is loud enough to burst our eardrums.

You can tell how old a whale is by digging out its ear wax – it has growth rings just like trees. Count the rings and you'll know how many years it's been alive.

50 million years ago, whales walked on four legs. Over the years they evolved to lose the legs, but modern whales still have a kind of pelvis (the middle part of your body to which your legs are attached) and are sometimes born with little back legs that they can't actually use.

The **narwhal** is a kind of whale found in the waters of the Arctic that has a unique feature – the males have a huge tusk, like a unicorn horn,

growing from their head that can be as long as 5.5 metres. This 'tusk' is actually a tooth that keeps growing all its life from the left side of its upper jaw. They use it like a sword to fight other creatures, and as a tool to break ice. In the medieval era, people would make cups from their tusks, believing that they magically prevented poisoning.

Wombats

Wombat poo is cube-shaped. The adorable animals leave these dry poop cubes around as a way of messaging each other and marking out their territory. The cube shape means that these 'messages' stay in one place, as the cubes can't roll away.

It's not just kangaroos that have pouches to keep their young in. Wombats keep their babies in pouches too, except their pouches are upside down. This actually makes sense, as it means that when the wombat is digging through the dirt, the dirt doesn't collect in the pouch with the baby.

Wombats have extremely tough bottoms. Their bums are as hard as rock, as they're made of four

layers of solid cartilage, fat, skin and fur.

If a predator approaches a wombat's burrow, the wombat will point his backside up out of the hole to plug the entrance, as it knows its bum is too tough for the predator to hurt.

Zebras

When they're young foals, zebras can have a black coat with white polka dots instead of stripes.

If you had a time machine, one fun thing to do would be to go back to London Zoo in the year 1914, where you could have a ride in a carriage pulled by zebras.

Did you know that you can barcode-scan a zebra? You can't use a supermarket scanner though, you have to use a special one called a StripeSpotter. Scientists built it so they can quickly identify different zebras in the wild and keep track of them.

When they're chased by lions, zebras **FART** with every step as they run away.

WHO'S THE SMARTEST?

Mammal Round

Play this game of true or false to find the smartest person in a group of your family or friends (or play it yourself to see how big your own brains are). Here's how it works: everyone playing the game stands up. Tell them to raise their hand if they think the answer is true. If they get it wrong, they have to sit down. The last person standing is the smartest! But be careful, there are some sneaky trick questions in here ...

1. True or false? The Arabic name for hamster translates as 'Mr Saddlebags'.

It's **TRUE**. Syrian hamsters, also called golden hamsters, were given the name because of their ability to stuff their cheeks with food.

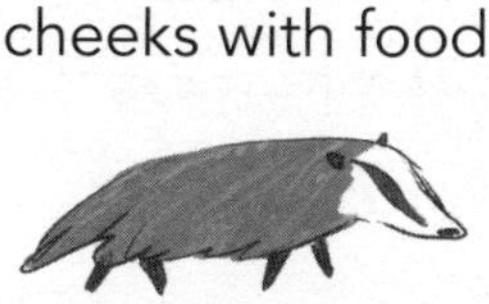

2. True or false? London Zoo used to hire camels to mow their lawns.

It's **TRUE**. A hundred years ago, camels were used to pull heavy lawnmowers to cut the grass at London Zoo. Horses were also used to pull early mowers, and to protect the grass from their sharp hooves they were sometimes fitted with leather boots.

3. True or false? There are kittens floating in the rings of the planet Saturn. Their names include Garfield, Sylvester, Socks, Fluffy and Whiskers.

It's **TRUE**. 'Kittens' are what NASA scientists called the 15,000 lumps of rock (which are also called minimoons or moonlets) that they've spotted drifting in the rings of dust that orbit Saturn.

4. True or false? Rottweiler dogs can purr like cats when they're happy.

It's **TRUE**. It's called the 'Rottie Rumble'.

5. True or false? The US Air Force hired a rabbit to help build a computer.

It's **FALSE** – it was actually a ferret! When US Space Command were building a base in Colorado, they needed to connect their computers with wires running down 12-mile-long tunnels, which were too small for a human to crawl down. So one of the airmen gave the job to his pet ferret Misty, who ran down the tunnels to the other end with the wire tied around her waist. After just an hour of work she was done, and was paid with her favourite treat: strawberry Pop-Tarts.

6. True or false? Bloodhounds use their ears to smell.

It's **TRUE**. Bloodhounds have long droopy ears that scoop up scents from the ground and sweep them towards their nostrils. Their wrinkles also help, trapping particles of the smells inside.

7. True or false? Sloths can hold their breath for as long as a dolphin can.

It's **FALSE**. Sloths can actually hold their breath for TWICE AS LONG as a dolphin, which can swim for about 20 minutes underwater before needing to come up for air. A sloth can last 40 minutes without air.

And while they're slow-moving on land, in water they can swim three times faster.

8. True or false? Tigers like to walk into water backwards.

It's **TRUE**. Tigers prefer to back into lakes and rivers as they hate to get their eyes wet, which is also why they swim with their heads above water.

9. True or false? Humpback dolphins like to juggle with sponges.

It's **TRUE**. Scientists have seen male dolphins along Australia's north-west coast rip sponges off the ocean floor and bring them up to the surface to play with them, throwing them up into the air and catching them to impress female dolphins. Sometimes, they'll toss them to the females as gifts.

10. True of false? Most cats are lactose intolerant and shouldn't be given milk.

It's **TRUE**. As kittens, they can happily drink their mother's milk, but as they get older, they lose the ability to digest milk.

INCREDIBLY
INTERESTING
INVERTEBRATES

You'd think animals with no spine or skeleton inside wouldn't even be able to get out of bed in the morning, let alone survive in the world for millions of years. But the fact is that **invertebrates**, which is the class of animal species that you can identify by this major lack of boniness, were the first animals to evolve on this planet – they've been around for a BILLION years.

They're also, by far, the biggest group of the six different classes of animals in this book. Today, invertebrates make up a brain-boggling 97 per cent of all animal species, and include worms, sponges, molluscs, octopuses, and a whole number of other families, like insects. We share the planet with a lot of insects. I mean, A LOT. For every person on Earth, there are 1.4 billion insects, and each year we discover about 10,000 new species. They devour about one tenth of the world's food supply. Nearly all of them are weird, but let's start with my favourite …

Ants

All ants are incredibly strong for their size – they can lift 100 times their body weight. If an ant was as big as a fox, for example, it could lift a cow over its head.

In the Central American country of Costa Rica, there are army ants that are very aggressive and deliver painful stings, but people use them to clean houses. If you let them into your home and leave them alone, they pick out all the dead insects in corners and bits of food on the floor and take them away, like miniature vacuum cleaners.

Ants can build huge homes for themselves. The largest ant colony that has ever been found was discovered in northern Spain in 2002. The series of connecting nests stretched across a total distance of 5,760 km. Several billion ants call this mega-colony home.

When intruders attack the nests of Brunei ants, they deliberately EXPLODE their own HEADS to confuse and slow down the invaders.

The **Australian bulldog ant** is one of the most venomous insects in the world, and is as stubborn as its name suggests – it can kill a human in just 15 minutes by biting with its powerful jaws and stinging over and over again until you collapse.

Bees

Only female bees can sting.

The most painful place a bee can sting you is inside your nostril. We know this because a man named Michael Smith let bees sting him on every part of his body, and wrote down which places hurt the most. (Scientists are weird sometimes.)

Next time you're looking out of an aeroplane window, keep an eye out for Alpine bumblebees – they can fly higher than Mount Everest.

In 2017, researchers at Nottingham Trent University discovered that every time honeybees bump into each other inside the hive, they make a loud WHOOP sound of surprise.

When they're thirsty, several types of bees get water by drinking the tears of larger animals.

You really wouldn't want to be an insect burglar in a honeybee hive. If they detect an intruder, honeybees will swarm all over it in a huge group and vibrate their bodies. These vibrations make so much heat that the burglar is literally **BAKED** to **DEATH**.

Daniel Wildman (fl.1771) was a London beekeeper and honey salesman who advertised his shop by riding around town on a horse in an unusual way – he stood upright on the saddle while wearing a beard of bees. He certainly lived up to his surname!

Beetles

Almost 25 per cent of all known animal species are beetles. In London's Natural History Museum, beetle specimens fill 22,000 drawers.

If you don't have any cotton buds lying around, there are other ways to clean your ears. The Korowai people of Western New Guinea stick the wriggling larvae of beetles in their ears to MUNCH on their earwax. (Just one of many things in this book that you absolutely should not try yourself.)

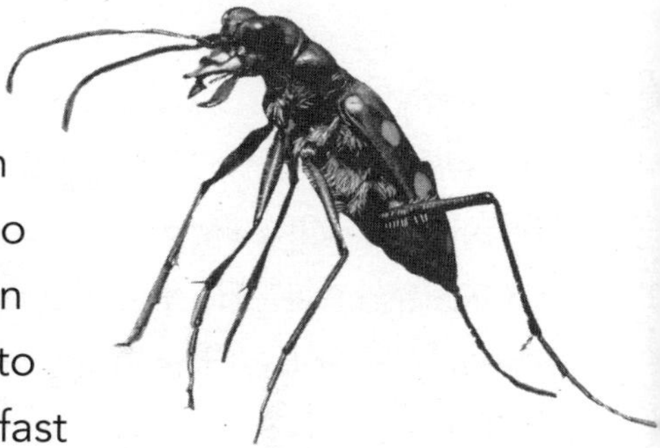

Tiger beetles run so quickly (with a top speed record of 9 km/h or 5.6 mph) that they go temporarily blind. When they sprint at full pace to chase prey, they go so fast that their brain can't work out where their victim is, and they have to stop and wait to get their sight back before beginning the chase again.

If you ever need to hide from predators, and you're really desperate, consider the trick of the potato beetle, which covers itself in its own poop to make

itself too disgusting to eat. Baby lily beetles do the same thing with their parents' poop to disguise themselves as bird droppings.

The **dung beetle** is the first known insect to use the stars to navigate. As it rolls a giant ball of dung around, which it eats, it uses the stars of the Milky Way to travel in a straight line, like sailors at sea.

The rhinoceros beetle is so powerful that if it was the same size as a man, it could raise nine elephants into the air in one go.

Butterflies

Butterflies' ears are on their wings. They even have eardrums, and are used by the butterfly to hear the ultrasound of bats, which like to eat butterflies as snacks.

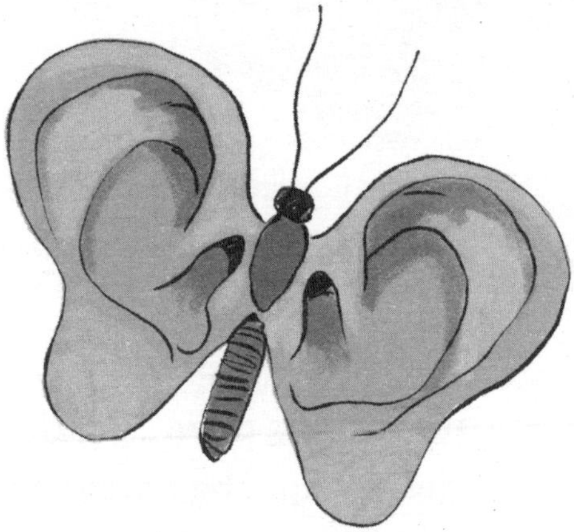

Caterpillars turn into butterflies, but here's a weird thing: caterpillars poop, but butterflies don't. In fact, caterpillars poop all the time, but when they turn into butterflies they don't eat and only drink.

Instead of pooping, they'll spray a small mist every now and then, which is almost pure water.

Butterflies' tongues aren't like ours – they're actually straws that they use to suck up liquids.

Butterflies drink the tears of turtles to get salt.

Clams

The biggest **giant clam** ever found on the planet was discovered under London – the fossilised remains of the monster clam showed that it was 2 metres wide.

The smallest species of giant clam is called the 'boring clam', which I think makes it rather interesting. The boring clam gets its name from its habit of boring, or drilling, holes in wood and stone. This of course was a major problem for sailors on wooden ships, who really don't like things making holes in their hulls! It's why boring clams were also called 'ship worms'.

The giant clam has hundreds of eyes along its body.

Cockroaches

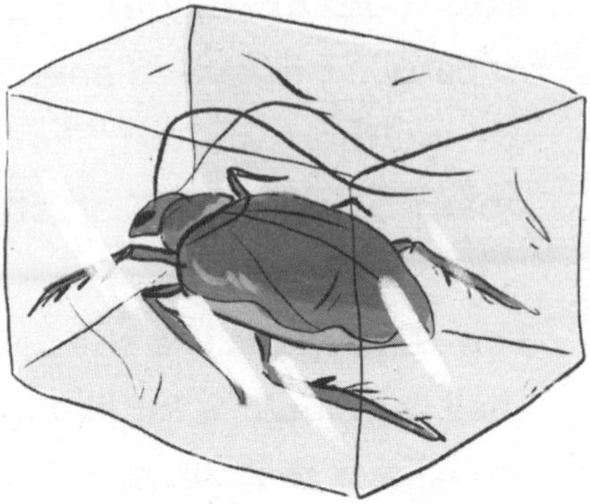

Cockroaches are some of the planet's toughest inhabitants. They can survive being frozen for two days, can hold their breath underwater for 40 minutes, can flatten themselves to the thickness of a sheet of paper to crawl through cracks and can even live for a week after losing their head!

One of the largest cockroaches on the planet is the ***Megaloblatta longipennis***, which can measure 9.7 cm long and 4.5 cm wide, with a wingspan of 20 cm.

Crabs

Coconut crabs grow to the size of dogs. They hunt birds and can climb trees.

Pom-pom crabs get their name from their habit of carrying fuzzy sea anemones in their claws and waving them around, like a cheerleader waves pom-poms, to scare off attackers.

The Heikegani is a species of Japanese crab with a shell that looks a lot like a human face. People used to believe that when samurai warriors died in battle, they were reincarnated (brought back to life in a new physical form) as these crabs, and many people today still refuse to eat them because of this.

The male Southeast Asian **mangrove crab** is so proud when he wins a fight against another male that he does an elaborate victory dance.

When they're frightened, sponge crabs hide themselves by sticking sea sponges on their heads.

The **yeti crab** was only discovered in 2005 in the South Pacific Ocean. It was named after the mythical yeti creature because of the huge amount of setae, or bristles, that cover its legs and claws, giving it the appearance of being furry.

Dragonflies

The eye of the dragonfly is an amazing piece of natural technology. While humans have one lens per eye, dragonflies have THOUSANDS of miniature lenses called ommatidia, which allow it to have a 360-degree field of vision. This means a dragonfly can see directly behind itself.

When animals travel a great distance to breed or search for a safer environment, it's called migration. The animal that travels the furthest when it migrates is a type of dragonfly. It's called the **globe skinner**, and it flies a whopping 11,000 miles back and forth over the Indian Ocean.

Dragonflies catch other insects by swooping down on them and grabbing them with their feet.

Today, most dragonflies have wingspans of only 5–13 cm, but we know from fossils that there were dragonflies that lived 300 million years ago (before dinosaurs) that had wingspans of around 76 cm. Scientists call them **griffinflies**.

When male and female dragonflies mate, their tails join to form a heart shape.

Flies

Flies have hairs in their feet that they use to taste what they're standing on. With these hairs, they are

10 million times better at detecting sugar than the human tongue.

You probably know spiders eat flies, but did you know there are flies which eat spiders? They're called hunchback flies. A female hunchback fly will spray out hundreds of eggs, some of which get stuck to aspider's abdomen. The young larvae wriggle into the body of the spider, then go to sleep. They may sleep for as long as three years inside the spider, but when they wake up, the now-grown hunchback flies will eat the spider from the inside out.

Houseflies buzz in the musical key of F major.

Gnats

What New Zealanders call glow worms are actually a type of gnat. They have a pretty clever way of catching other insects – they hang around high up in the roofs of caves, like the Waitomo Cave on

New Zealand's North Island, and use their glow to pretend to be shining stars in the night sky. When other insects fly towards them, they get tangled in their dangling silk threads, allowing the glow worms to eat them.

Jellyfish

Jellyfish don't have brains, hearts or bones. Some, like the **box jellyfish**, have 24 eyes. Several of these eyes always look up towards the sky, even when the jellyfish is upside down.

As well as the stingers in their tentacles, which can stun or even kill other animals, jellyfish can also defend themselves by SHOOTING MUCUS (which is basically snot) at lobsters, like a giant sneeze. Lobsters try to fight this by using their legs as windscreen wipers.

Danish scientists have made jellyfish crisps that taste like delicious pork scratchings. There is also an ice-cream company called 'Lick Me I'm Delicious' that has made jellyfish ice cream that glows in the dark when you lick it. One scoop costs £140.

There is a jellyfish called the fried egg jellyfish because it, er, looks exactly like a fried egg. It spends most of its time floating perfectly still, letting its prey enter its mouthlike openings. Sometimes, small animals like crabs will hitch a ride on top of it, safe from its stingers below.

The **lion's mane jellyfish** (*Cyanea capillata*) is one of the longest animals in the world. The largest example ever found had tentacles measuring 36.6 metres in length, which is the height of the average lighthouse.

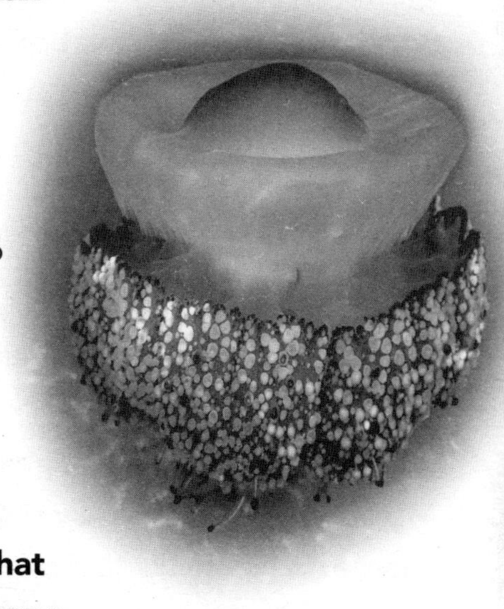

Some jellyfish never die – their life cycle means that they revert to their younger form as polyps, and begin their life over again. That doesn't mean they can't be killed, but if they avoid predators and disease, then theoretically they can live forever.

Jellyfish were around before dinosaurs.

Ladybirds

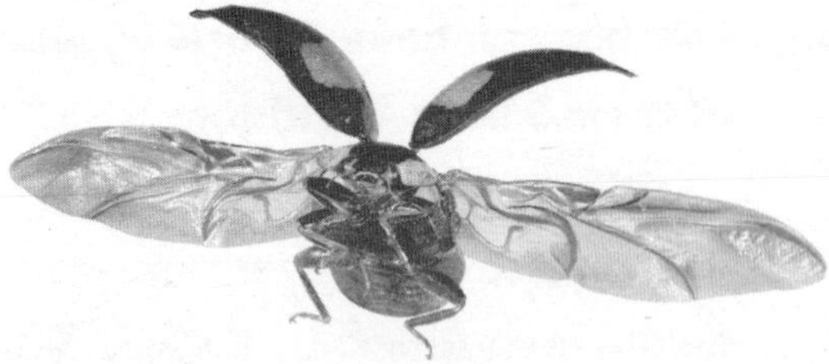

Ladybirds can fly as fast as racehorses can run.

We used to think that ladybirds were quite low-flyers, but then we spotted ladybirds flying as high as 1,100 metres. They've been known to travel as far as 74 miles in a single trip.

While humans are good at telling each other apart by recognising faces, ladybirds recognise each other by smelling each other's feet.

The wings of a ladybird are four times longer than its whole body.

There are more species of ladybirds than there are species of mammals.

Leeches

After latching on to your skin, leeches will only stop drinking blood when they've bloated to five times their original size. You don't feel their bite because it carries a natural painkiller.

Leeches can have 32 brains, with 100 teeth in each of their 3 jaws. Shudder.

The largest leech ever discovered was an Amazon giant leech found by Dr Roy Sawyer in French Guiana in the 1970s. He named it 'Grandma Moses'. She was 45 cm long (the same size as a one-year-old kitten) and had 750 babies.

Limpets

If a starfish tries to attack a limpet (a type of aquatic snail), smaller limpets will move out of the way, but larger limpets will stay and fight. They lift up their shell and then STAMP it down on the starfish's arm, scaring it away.

A limpet can run away from a threat at a top speed of 5 cm per hour.

One of the hardest materials in the whole world can be found in the mouth of the limpet sea

snails – its row of tiny teeth are made from a material called goethite, which contains iron. The teeth are 100 times thinner than a human hair and razor sharp. They allow the limpet to bite into rocks to avoid being swept away by waves.

Lobsters

A lobster can live for as long as a week out of water, as long as it's kept moist.

One in 2 million lobsters is born bright blue. One in 30 million is born bright yellow.

If they lose an eye, lobsters can regrow it. They can only do this a few times – if they lose an eye one too many times, they'll grow a limb instead. Lobsters can swim backwards, but they can't swim forwards.

Lobsters aren't fussy eaters – they even eat themselves. When they shed their skin, they'll devour it for all the calcium it contains.

Mosquitoes

Only female mosquitoes suck blood. You are extra attractive to a mosquito if you've recently eaten a banana or are wearing dark-coloured clothing.

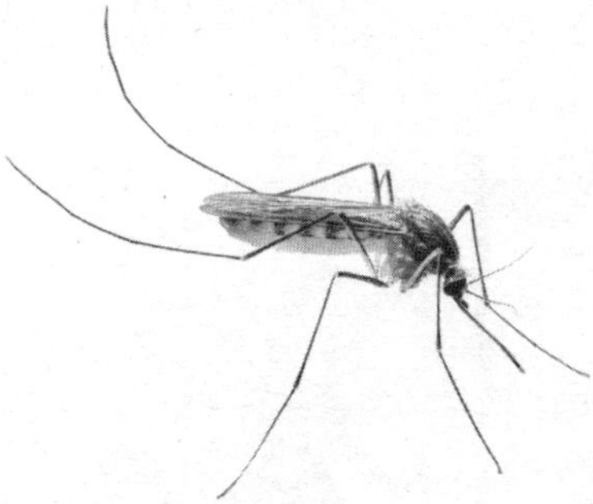

When a male and female mosquito are attracted to each other, they synchronise their wing beats to match each other.

Mosquitoes are our greatest enemy. About 108 billion human beings have lived on this planet since our species began, and nearly half of them – 52 billion people – have been killed by the ***Anopheles* mosquito**. Its bite carries the *Plasmodium* parasite, which infects humans with the deadly disease malaria.

Moths

The largest moth in the world is the Hercules moth, which has a wingspan of up to 36 cm. The Hercules spends as much as two years in its cocoon, but after it emerges it only lives for as long as two to eight days. This is because it's born without a mouth, and so dies of starvation.

A third of all pollination on the planet is done by moths.

The n'gwa caterpillar is so poisonous that hunters in Africa have stuck them onto the tips of their arrows and spears to make them deadly.

Before it becomes a moth, the **polyphemus caterpillar** spends its first 56 days eating 86,000 times its own weight in food – in human terms, this is like a newborn baby eating 2,678 burgers every day.

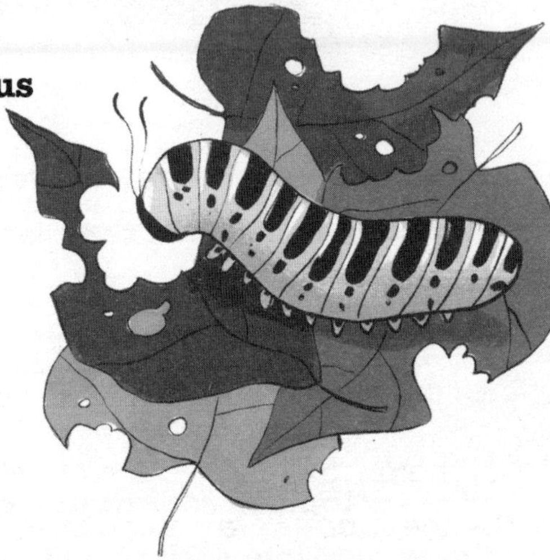

The greater wax moth has the greatest hearing range of any creature on Earth – it can hear the high-pitched noises made by bats, which allows it to hide from them, but it can also make its own noises that are so high-pitched that even bats can't hear them.

Octopus

Octopuses come in wildly different sizes – some are just 2 cm wide, others are 6 metres across.

Dumbo octopuses are so called because of their large ear-like fins that they use to swim.

Octopuses can taste things through the suction cups on their tentacles.

When octopuses are irritated with each other they throw sand into each other's faces. The gloomy octopus throws seashells at its enemy. Octopuses have been seen carrying around coconut shells in case a fight breaks out and they need a weapon.

Octopuses don't like being teased by humans. One scientist teased an octopus to see what would happen, and when he came back the next day, the octopus squirted him in the face with ink. It turned out that the octopus had been so angry from the teasing that it had spent hours doing target practice.

Octopolis and Octlantis are the names given to two different underwater areas off the coast of Australia where gloomy octopuses gather together to socialise, even though they normally like to be by themselves. It's thought that occasionally going to these octopus parties helps the animals grow smarter.

The **larger Pacific striped octopus**, also known as the **harlequin octopus**, catches its prey by sneaking up behind it and tapping it on the shoulder. The prey is so startled that it swims straight into the octopus's waiting tentacles and open mouth.

Scorpions

Scorpions were here before the first dinosaurs. About 450 million years ago, there were scorpions roaming the sea that may have been more than 1 metre long.

Scorpions glow under UV light. We're not sure why.

Scorpions can go without food for up to a whole year.

Sea Cucumbers

The garlic bread sea cucumber (yup, that's a real animal) lives off the shores of Singapore, and is exactly what it sounds like. Shaped like a loaf with tube-like feet along its body, it can grow up to 40 cm long and weigh 1.5 kg.

Sea Urchins

Sea urchins can **CHEW** through **ROCK** without damaging their teeth.

The red sea urchin lives in the Pacific Ocean off the coast of North America. It can live for up to 200 years in the wild. We used to think that this

was one of longest-living creatures on the planet until we discovered the glass sponge, which can live for about 15,000 years.

Sea urchins have ten feet.

Clownfish deliberately rub against the poisonous spines of the flower urchin, the most dangerous of all urchins, in order to build up immunity to its venom. Once they achieve this, they can eat the parasites on the urchin without risk of death.

Sea urchins have been spotted wearing dead **hermit crabs** as HATS.

Slugs And Snails

Slugs and snails have more teeth than sharks – they grind their food between a single jaw and a flexible band called a radula, that holds thousands of microscopic teeth. Using a microphone you can't hear slugs and snails move, but you can hear them eat.

Snails can regrow their eyes.

Slugs have four noses.

New Zealand has giant snails called **Powelliphanta**, which can grow to the size of hamburgers. They have beautiful pink shells, and eat insects, worms and other snails.

Snails can walk upside down along the underside of the surface of water.

Snails can take naps that last for up to three years.

If you see a snail slime trail on the ground, it doesn't mean that just one snail has passed by, it could be a whole lot more. Snails sometimes follow the slime trails of others as the greasy route means they only have to use a third of the mucus they normally would to travel, and about 35 times less energy! The slime doesn't just serve a purpose for movement, it also protects the snail from sharp objects and edges – a snail can slide across the sharp edge of a razorblade without getting cut thanks to its slime.

Spiders

The silk that spiders make is stronger than steel. Scientists have made bulletproof skin from spider silk.

The bird-dung crab spider probably isn't popular at parties – not only does it look like a pile of bird poop, but it also smells like it too – this helps attract flies that it grabs and eats.

Jumping spiders are able to make deadly accurate leaps to capture prey. They jump far, too – the ***Colonus puerperus*** in the eastern United States can jump 38 times the length of its body. Another freaky detail about jumping spiders? The males have fangs that are longer than their entire bodies.

Tarantulas can't spin webs.

The **Goliath birdeater** is a tarantula and the largest spider in the world, weighing 175 g and measuring around 13 cm long. The largest one ever found was in Venezuela and measured 28 cm across.

Some spiders can fly. Balloon spiders throw silk threads up into the sky, which get picked up by the wind and pull the spiders up with them. (Scientists call this 'ballooning', but really a more accurate term would be 'kiting'.)

Ant spiders are so called because they hunt ants by pretending to be ants – they lift their two front legs up into the air and wave them around to make them look like ant antennae.

There are at least five species of spider that are so powerful that they can catch and eat fish (the fish are usually twice the size of the spider).

Spiders find it really easy to climb walls because they have around 600,000 micro-hairs on their legs that cling to the wall. These hairs are so strong that a spider could technically carry something that is 170 times its own weight without falling. This would be like Spiderman climbing up a wall with 170 people on his back.

Squid

The eyes of the giant squid are the size of basketballs.

The giant squid's brain is weird for two reasons: one, it's shaped like a doughnut, and two, this doughnut-shaped brain is wrapped around its throat. This means if it tries to swallow something too large for its throat, it can give itself brain damage.

The feeding tentacles of the giant squid, which it uses to grab prey, can be as long as 10 metres, which is about the same length as a London double-decker bus.

There's a squid with one small eye and one giant eye – it's called the **cock-eyed squid**.

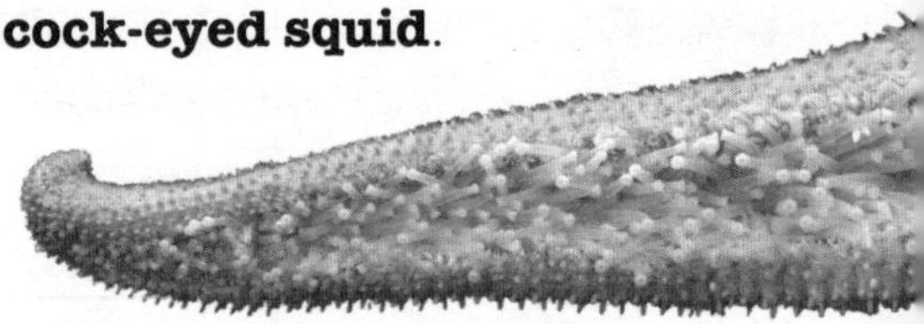

Starfish

Starfish have eyes at the ends of their arms.

In 2023, scientists at the University of Southampton found that the entire body of a starfish is actually its head. It's thought that they evolved to shed their body over time.

The **sunflower sea star** is a starfish that starts life with five arms, but by the time it's an adult it has as many as 24 arms. As beautiful as they are, resembling flowers in colours of orange and purple, they are meat-eating predators, gobbling up sea urchins, clams and sea snails at the bottom of the north-east Pacific Ocean.

Termite

There is a species of termite in the South American region of French Guiana that grows sacs of toxic blue liquid on its abdomen. If intruders try to enter their nest, this termite will deliberately explode to save its friends, covering its enemies in poison.

If you play them loud music, termites eat twice as fast.

In South Africa, you can buy roasted termites to eat like popcorn.

The termite queen will lay one egg every second, which is hard work considering she lives for about 50 years (unlike the worker termites who probably won't live more than two years).

Cathedral termites build enormous homes out of mud, chewed-up wood, spit and their own poop. They even build little mushroom gardens for these houses so that they have food supplies. Some of these cathedral termite mounds are as tall as a (human) three-storey house.

Wasps

Wasps recognise each other's faces.

If an ant is trying to get at food that a wasp wants, the annoyed wasp will pick up the ant, fly it away and drop it. Luckily for the ant, it's so small that it can survive a fall from any height.

It's not just bees that make honey – some wasps do, too. The **Mexican honey wasp** makes edible honey that is considered a delicacy by the people of the Popoloca town of Los Reyes Metzontla, Mexico, who also eat the wasps as snacks.

Worms

The tobacco hornworm uses its awful stinky breath to stop predators eating it.

Earthworms have five hearts. The worms 'breathe' through their skin, absorbing oxygen into their blood which these hearts then pump around the body.

The biggest tapeworm that has ever been found inside a human body was 35 metres long.

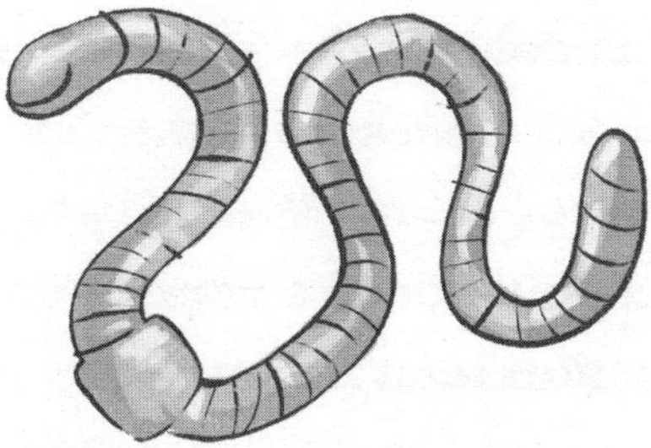

The **green bomber worm**, or **bombardier** worm, is a translucent sea worm that lives deep in the Pacific Ocean, where sunlight doesn't reach it. It has a trick to fool predators – it releases its gills to act like decoys. The gills glow green and float around like a shoal of small fish, which confuses the predator, giving the worm enough time to swim away.

Railroad worms aren't actually worms, but beetle larvae. Weirdly, they look like traffic lights – their bodies glow green while their heads glow red.

The **bootlace worm** can be found along the British coastline, and you'd know it if you saw it – it may only be 5–10 millimetres wide but it can grow up to 55 metres long, which is longer than an Olympic-size swimming pool. Not that you'd particularly want to, but don't touch it. The mucus it releases when scared is very poisonous and stinks of sewage.

Worms don't have tongues but they do have cells all around their body to taste and smell the soil around them. That means that if you pick up a worm, it's tasting your fingers.

WHO'S THE SMARTEST?

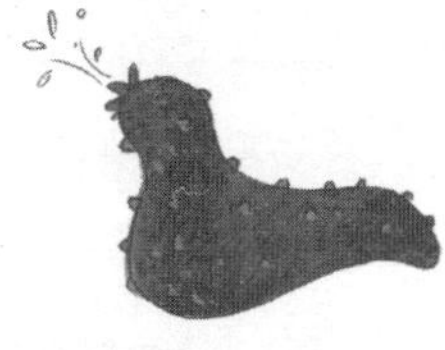

Invertebrate Round

1. True or false? There's a species of Australian wasp called the 'Hee Hee Hee'.

It's **FALSE**. It's actually called the 'Aha ha' wasp. It was named by a scientist called Arnold Menke in 1977, when he found it inside a package and, excited to find a new species, shouted 'AHA!' to which another scientist replied 'Ha!' He was so proud of his discovery that he even changed his car's licence plate to 'AHA HA'.

2. True or false? Sea urchins don't have eyes, but they can still see.

It's **TRUE**. They sense light with their spines. They're the only creatures known to be able to do this.

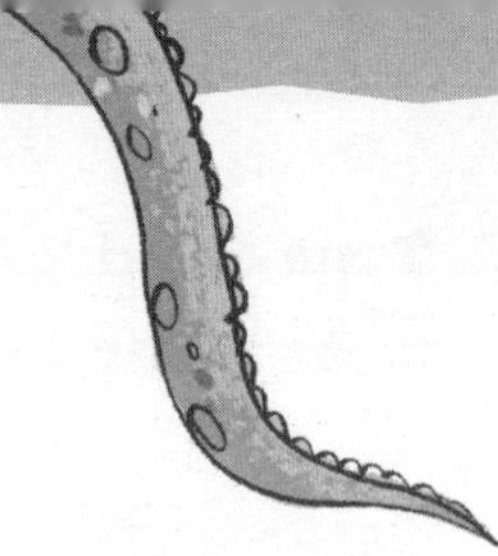

3. True or false? An octopus can unscrew a jam jar in just two minutes.

It's **FALSE**. They can open a jar even faster! An octopus in New Zealand called Ozy set a world record for octopus-jar-opening in 2014 when he unscrewed a jar to get to a treat inside in just 54 seconds.

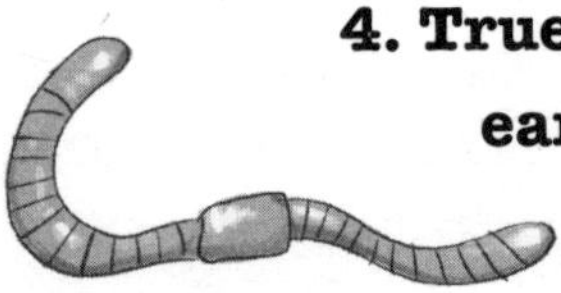

4. True or false? When two earthworms mate, they both get pregnant.

It's **TRUE**. Seems like a fairer way of doing things, no?

5. True or false? 'Sparkle-muffin' is an ancient name for a unicorn.

It's **FALSE**. Sparkle-muffins are alive today and are a colourful kind of Australian jumping spider. The male shows off to the female by puffing himself up and waving his colourful flaps around. If she's not impressed, she eats him.

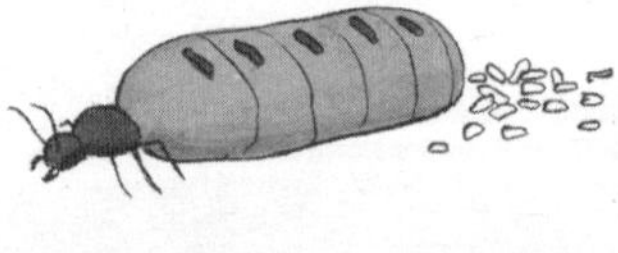

6. True or false? The puss caterpillar gets its name for being as big as a cat.

It's **FALSE**. In fact, the 2.5-centimetre-long puss caterpillar, which lives in the USA, Mexico and Central America, is named for its grey-brown 'fur'. This sounds adorable, but the 'fur' is actually a load of sharp spines. People who have been poked by them say that it's more painful than breaking a bone or touching something white-hot.

7. True or false? Crickets can tell you the temperature.

It's **TRUE**. Crickets chirp more frequently the warmer the weather is. If you count the number of chirps in 15 seconds and then add 40, you will likely get the temperature in Fahrenheit, give or take a few degrees. (Bonus fact: crickets hear through their knees.)

8. True or false? You only need 50 fireflies to make enough light to read this book in the dark.

It's **FALSE** – fireflies shine so brightly that you would only need six of them!

9. True or false? If a flea was the size of a human it could jump over the Houses of Parliament in London.

It's **TRUE** – not only that, but a flea is such a powerful jumper that a human-sized flea could jump over two Houses of Parliament stacked on top of each other.

10. True or false? There's an insect that can turn you into a vegetarian.

It's **TRUE**. Just one bite from the lone star tick (found in USA and Mexico) can make you allergic to meat for the rest of your life.

FASCINATINGLY
FREAKY FISH

You might think you know a **fish** when you see one, but it can be tricky to say exactly what a fish is. Technically speaking, they're cold-blooded, they don't have arms or legs, they breathe through their gills and they're vertebrates (have spines). But some fish, as we'll see, break these rules. And here's another odd thing – birds, frogs, lizards, turtles and mammals (including you) all evolved from fish. Millions and millions of years ago, our ancestor was a fish. So, wait, am I a fish? Are you a fish? Is your dog a fish?

It's so complicated that some scientists say that there's no such thing as a 'fish' because there are just too many different animals covered by that word. Which is great for this book, because it means we've got a seriously weird variety of things to cover ...

Have you ever wondered how we measure the speed of a swimming fish? It's really difficult to record (police radar guns don't work too well in the ocean). The best way is to measure how fast they unspool a fishing reel after they've been hooked on the end and swim away in a panic. **Sailfish**

hold the fish speed record – they've pulled over 90 metres of line out in just 3 seconds.

Fish can't talk, of course, but recently scientists discovered that some fish can communicate by FARTING. In 2003, biologists investigating a mysterious underwater sound realised it was caused by bubbles blown out of a herring's bottom. No fish had ever been known to make sounds from its bottom before.

Humans like to sunbathe to relax, and fish do too – **ocean sunfish** float at the water's surface to feel the Sun's rays on their backs. It's thought they do this to store up the heat, so that they're cosy when diving down into the cold depths of the ocean later.

If you give a fish enough prawn-cocktail-flavoured crisps to eat, it can turn them pink! We know this because workers at London's Sea Life Aquarium were worried their giant gourami fish called Gerty wasn't eating. Then they discovered that her previous owner had given her Skips and it was the only thing she liked. She ate so many that she turned pink.

Every summer the inhabitants of Yoro, Honduras, hold a festival called the *Festival de Lluvia de Peces* ('festival of the fish rain') in the hope that fish will fall from the sky.

When they have to escape through a narrow gap in an emergency, fish form an orderly queue.

380 million years ago, fish had finger bones.

Anchovies

You might have heard of sabre-toothed tigers, but how about sabre-toothed fish? Scientists have found two fossilised examples in Belgium and Pakistan of sabre-toothed anchovies that lived 55 million years ago. The fearsome fish were 1 metre long, and had one huge sabre tooth at the front of the mouth.

Anglerfish

Anglerfish are found on the dark sea floors around the world, but all have the same distinctive trick to lure their prey towards them. They use a fin ray that grows from

the centre of their forehead, shaped a bit like a fishing rod, which dangles a ball of glowing bacteria like a lure in front of their open mouth full of very sharp teeth. When smaller fish approach, it strikes.

Batfish

The red-lipped batfish might just be one of the most glamorous inhabitants of the waters around the Galapagos Islands, thanks to their – yup, you guessed it – bright red lips, which make them look like they've applied a thick layer of lipstick. It's thought this feature is to help them stand out when spawning (releasing eggs).

Bony-eared assfish

The brain of the bony-eared assfish is so small that it weighs one thousandth of its total weight. (Bonus points if you somehow managed to not giggle at its name.)

Catfish

There's a small catfish in the waters of Africa's Central Congo River basin which swims upside down. It's called the upside-down catfish. Its unusual technique makes it easier to eat insects on the water's surface.

The male **hardhead catfish** is a devoted father – he'll carry up to 48 eggs around in his mouth until they hatch, to make sure predators don't get them. So how does he eat during all that time? He doesn't!

Celebes medaka

The Celebes medaka is a strange Indonesian species of fish that turns black when it gets angry. Its dark markings appear within a minute of fighting, as a way of scaring its enemy. This kind of colour change ability is seen in another fish, too: the eyes of the Trinidadian guppy, for example, will turn black when it's preparing to attack a rival.

Clownfish

Clownfish (think Nemo and his dad from Disney's *Finding Nemo*) begin life as males, but can turn into females when they mature. In their hierarchy, there

is always a female in charge – if she dies, one of the males will change into a female to take her place.

Croakers

Some fish are so noisy it can be dangerous to swim near them. Scientists studied a huge shoal of fish called croakers in the Gulf of California, and heard the fish making sounds by drumming their stomach muscles against their swim bladders. The result was a deafening noise like a machine gun. Divers are told to avoid the area as the noise could be dangerous to them. 'IT'S AS LOUD AS A LAWNMOWER OR CHAINSAW,' **shouted one scientist while rubbing his ears.**

Eels

Sure, you wouldn't want to get too near one, and they aren't going to win any beauty pageants, but

how cool is the **electric eel**? Its special organs allow it to release an electric shock of up to 650 volts (which is nearly three times the power of the wall sockets in your house). It could use this weapon to be a bully, but it doesn't – it only releases the jolt to keep predators away and to stun prey.

Electric eels aren't actually eels – they're a kind of knifefish, and are more closely related to catfish than eels.

Lucius Licinius Crassus (140–91 BCE) was a Roman politician who loved his pet eel so much that he gave it necklaces and earrings, and held a huge funeral for it when it died.

Flying Fish

Flying fish don't actually fly – not in the way that birds do anyway – but what they can do is just as amazing. They LEAP out of the water and use their long wing-like fins to glide on the wind to escape predators chasing them. They can jump 6 metres

up into the air, and have been seen gliding as far as 400 metres, which is the same length as the Eiffel Tower lying on its side.

As you might expect, when they're gliding through the air flying fish are pretty vulnerable to attacks from birds above. Young flying fish have a kind of disguise, using strings of material called filaments that dangle from their lower jaws to make them look like plant blossoms.

Goldfish

Goldfish can grow a lot bigger than the little ones you see in fish tanks. The biggest goldfish ever recorded was named Carrot. Carrot weighed 30.5 kg, about the same weight and size as a one-year-old German shepherd dog.

If you stay at the Hotel Charleroi in Belgium and you feel lonely in your room, you can rent a goldfish for the night for company.

The Italian poet Gabriele D'Annunzio (1868–1938) made sure that all of his books were printed on

rubber, so that he could read them while he lazed in the enormous garden bath that he shared with his goldfish.

Hagfish

At first glance, hagfish look like eels – grey, tube-shaped and wriggly. But they are so much grosser than you can imagine. Mainly this is to do with their slime. The mucus (snot) glands in their skin can release a huge amount of this milky, thick slime when they are attacked by a predator. The slime is so thick that it blocks their attacker's gills, causing it to choke and letting the hagfish escape. The slime can be so thick that even the hagfish itself can drown in it.

Hagfish are the only known animal to have a skull but no backbone.

In Korea, hagfish are barbecued fresh and eaten in stir-fry dishes.

Handfish

Australia's red handfish have hand-like fins that they use to crawl along the sea floor, rather than

swim. Their 'hands' also make them very skilful at pouncing on prey.

Handfish are also known as 'warty anglers', as they have a special dorsal fin ray that dangles like a fishing line in front of their mouths. Unlike other fish that have this, though, the handfish can't use it to lure prey into its jaws, so it doesn't serve much purpose.

Killifish

The mangrove killifish of the western Atlantic is the only fish that lives in trees. It can survive for as long as two months on land. It crosses land by 'tail flipping', which is basically a jumping forward somersault. It uses holes made by insects to climb into trees, and lives there until it's time to go back to the ocean.

Manta Rays

Manta rays treat coral reefs like beauty salons. They go there to let the local fish eat the parasites off their skin.

The largest manta rays can be 2.1 metres wide, and weigh 2 tonnes! While they have about 300 sharp teeth, these are tiny and wouldn't be able to break your skin. In fact, the manta ray isn't a danger to you at all – if it feels even slightly threatened, it simply turns and flees.

Manta rays never stop swimming – they have to keep moving to stay alive, as the movement washes water over their gills which is how they get their oxygen.

Mudskippers

Just like the killifish, some species of fish can walk on land. Mudskippers grow up to 30 cm long and can spend several days out of water to cross land and even climb mangroves. Their side pectoral fins allow them to crawl, skip, climb and even leap a distance of 61 cm with the use of their tail.

Parrotfish

Every night, parrotfish make their own pyjamas. They **BURP** out mucus for about an hour, which coats the fish in a protective layer that wraps their entire body. Then in the morning, they eat it for breakfast.

Parrotfish eat coral and poo sand. Scientists think that as much as 70 per cent of the white sandy beaches of the Caribbean and Hawaii are made of sand pooed out by parrotfish. A single large adult parrotfish can produce over a tonne of sand in one year.

Pearlfish

The oceans are a dangerous place to live, so you can't blame a fish for choosing an unusual hiding place to be safe. The pearlfish certainly isn't fussy about where it lives – it swims right up a sea cucumber's **BOTTOM** and lives inside it during the day. At night, it leaves its living home to explore. The sea cucumber breathes through its bottom, so it can't close its bum to stop this happening, it just has to let the pearlfish come and go.

Perch

In the canals of the Dutch city of Utrecht, perch and other fish can't swim through the canal locks (which are large wooden gates in the water). So the people of Utrecht put in a live web-streaming camera, and a 'fish doorbell', which let people around the world watch the water over the internet. Whenever someone sees a fish waiting to go through the lock, that person can press the 'doorbell' button on their

computer screen, the lock will open and the fish can go through.

Piranhas

Piranha comes from the word *pi'rãia*, which means 'tooth fish' in the Brazilian language Tupí. Piranhas can replace their fearsome teeth several times over its lifetime, which helps keep them nice and sharp …

The piranha fish can make three different kinds of angry noise. When making eye contact with other piranha, it BARKS to say 'don't mess with me'. When it fights another piranha, it lets out a low grunt or thud sound to intimidate it. The third sound is probably the most frightening – if the rival fish won't swim away, the piranha charges at it, loudly GNASHING its huge teeth.

Despite their scary reputation, some piranhas are vegetarians, living off seeds and plants. In the Amazonian Trombetas basin in Pará, Brazil, for example, scientists found a species of piranha called ***Tometes camunani*** that only eats riverweeds.

Pufferfish

Pufferfish naturally contain one of the most deadly poisons in the animal kingdom, enough to kill three adult humans. Despite this, one kind of pufferfish called fugu is served as food in restaurants in Japan and Korea. To be a fugu chef, you have to train for three years to make sure you're good enough to not poison your customers.

Devils Hole pupfish

You can only find the Devils Hole pupfish in one place in the entire world: a water-filled cavern 130 metres deep, in the US state of Nevada. It's thought that the fish have been living there alone for as long as 60,000 years.

Sarcastic fringeheads

Sarcastic fringeheads are small fish found off the Pacific coast of North America. They get their strange name for the surprisingly aggressive behaviour of the males when dealing with a rival. They throw open their jaws about four times as wide as their body, and flash the bright colour of

the inside of their mouth. They then press their open mouths against each other in a kissing motion, until finally one is able to bite the other and scare them off.

Seahorses

With seahorses, it's the males that get pregnant. They give birth to anywhere between 12 to 1,000 babies. Seahorses greet their partners every morning with a dance. Scientists think this is their way of showing each other how in love they are.

Seahorse couples also hold each other's tail while they swim through seagrass so they don't get separated.

A seahorse can move its eyes in different directions simultaneously.

Seahorses are adorably slow swimmers. The lined seahorse, for example, which is 15 cm long, would take a full five minutes to swim the length of your bathtub.

When it comes to eating, however, seahorses don't waste any time – they snap their heads up so fast to grab food that scientists can only watch it happen by

using special high-speed cameras. They're also very accurate – they catch their prey about 94 per cent of the time, which is nearly as good as the most efficient hunter, the dragonfly, which has a success rate of about 95 per cent.

Sharks

Sharks are older than trees. The earliest tree species, the now-extinct *Archaeopteris*, grew around 350 million years ago in forests where we now find the Sahara Desert. Sharks have been around much longer – at least 400 million years.

Sharks have dimples along their snouts and flanks, which are 'electroreceptors'. These help them to detect the electric fields of the muscles of their prey. This means they can find food even in pitch-darkness.

The biggest fish in the world is the whale shark – the longest one ever spotted was 19 metres long, which is about the length of a bowling lane.

The **megamouth shark** is found all over the world, but was only discovered in 1976 when one got tangled in the anchor chain of a US Navy ship in Hawaii. Its **HUGE** mouth makes up half its head! The longest known megamouth measured 7 metres, which is actually larger than a **great white shark**, but on average they're about 5.5 metres long, which is the height of an adult giraffe. Its large mouth helps it scoop up lots of its primary food, plankton.

The horn shark has a colourful grin – it eats so many sea urchins that they stain its teeth beetroot-purple.

The pink-skinned **goblin shark** is one of those rare species that is so old it looks almost alien. Its chief weirdo feature is its terrifying jaws, which shoot forward from its head to snatch prey that probably thought it was at a safe distance. It's sometimes called a 'living fossil', as it is the only remaining member of the family *Mitsukurinidae*, a species of deep-sea creature that is about 125 million years old. It's very unusual to ever see one, as they live in the deepest parts of the ocean, but one captured in 2000 was a real monster – it measured about 6 metres long.

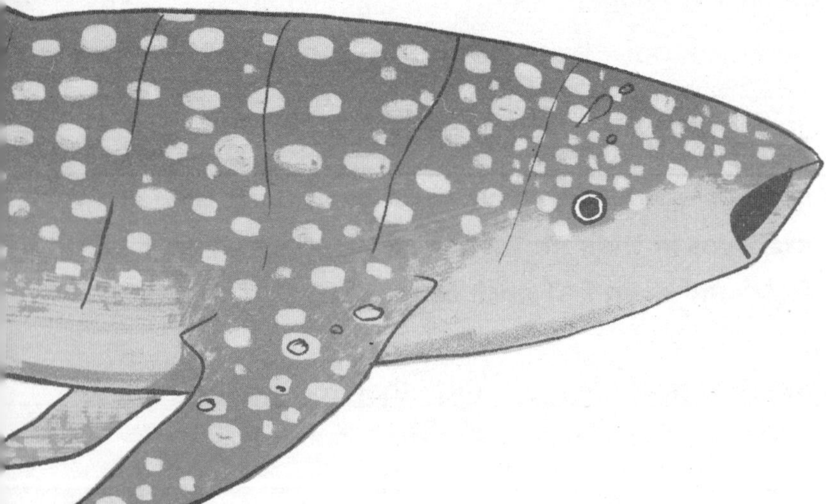

Greenland sharks are relatively slow swimmers (its top speed is 1.6 mph), so they have a natural defence against predators who might be thinking of eating them: their flesh is poisonous. If a human eats it, it can give you extreme stomach problems. However, when the meat is dried, it's safe for humans to eat – in Iceland, it's eaten as a special treat.

Greenland sharks are the longest-living vertebrates on Earth. Scientists testing the age of sharks in the North Atlantic found a female Greenland shark that was about 400 years old. (That discovery was in 2016, so if she's still alive she's even older today.) Greenland sharks are scavengers, which means they will eat anything they find. Scientists looking inside their stomachs have found the remains of reindeer, seals and even polar bears.

Some shark species are aggressive from the earliest of ages – before they've even been born, as tiny embryos in their mother's womb, shark siblings will fight and even EAT each other.

Shark attacks are much rarer than most people think. Scientists found that in America more people die

from a cow attack than a shark attack. Great white sharks can go three months without eating – but you don't want to be the first thing it sees after those three months!

Sunfish

Ocean sunfish produce 300 million eggs at once – they reproduce so rarely that when they do, they make it count.

Tigerfish

The **African tigerfish** can leap out of the water and grab birds in mid-air!

Triggerfish

The official fish of Hawaii is the *humuhumunukunukuāpua'a,* which means 'triggerfish with a snout like a pig'. When it flees predators, it grunts like a pig, probably to warn others.

Tripodfish

The tripodfish, *Bathypterois grallator*, has three rigid fin 'legs' that it uses to stand at the bottom of the ocean. It waits for its prey to swim close, and when it does, the tripodfish **KICKS** the creature into its mouth.

WHO'S THE SMARTEST?

Fish Round

1. True or false? Fish can get seasick.

It's **TRUE**. This was discovered by a German scientist called Dr Reinhold Hilbig in 2009, when he put 49 fish in an aeroplane and noticed that whenever the plane made a steep dive the fish got dizzy, and behaved just like seasick humans.

2. True or false? Fish can sneeze.

It's **FALSE**. Fish don't have the ability to sneeze, **BUT** they can cough. They do this to clear out bacteria from their gills.

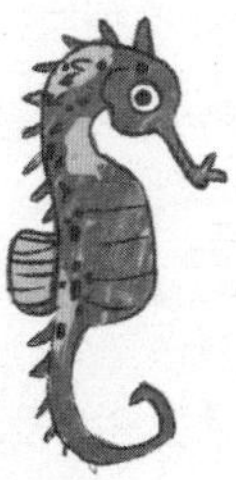

3. True or false? Seahorses can change their colour like chameleons.

It's **TRUE**. Seahorses can change colour when they want to hide from predators, and also when they want to show off to another

seahorse they like. Different pigments of colour are held in little sacs in their skin, and when they flex their muscles, they change their colour.

4. True or false? Female great white sharks give birth upside down.

It's **FALSE** … at least, as far as we know. Amazingly, no one has ever seen great white sharks mate or give birth. We think this is because they dive deep down into the Pacific Ocean to do this away from anything that might be a danger to their babies.

5. True or false? You can fit hundreds of Japan pigs in your hands.

It's **TRUE**. The Japan pig is otherwise known as the Japanese pygmy seahorse, which is the size of a jelly bean.

6. True or false? Monkfish and goosefish make surprisingly great pets.

It's **FALSE**. In fact, they're both different names for the same deep-sea fish that looks so evil that scientists nicknamed it the 'sea-devil'. Growing as large as 1.4 metres long, with their ultra-wide mouths they can swallow prey as large as themselves.

7. True or false? Every summer, a huge number of male great hammerhead sharks gather in the tropical waters of French Polynesia.

It's **FALSE**. The shark assembly does happen, but the hammerheads are all female. Normally the animals like to keep to themselves, but it's thought that they're all attracted by the full moon.

8. True or false? There is a fish from Madagascar that's older than Madagascar.

It's **TRUE**. The coelacanth is a 'living fossil' because of how old it is (over 420 million years). We used to think they were extinct until fishermen began catching them in their nets in 1938.

9. True or false? The 'ghost shark' doesn't exist.

It's **TRUE**. Technically speaking, there is no such fish because the creature known as the ghost shark is actually a kind of ratfish called the pointy-nosed blue chimaera. You can find it at a depth of one mile off the coast of Central California.

10. And finally ... which of these animal names have been made up?

The unicorn cod
The squirrelfish
The waspfish
The armoured sea robin
The sea bat
The wolf herring
The gobbleguts
The ponyfish

It's a **TRICK**. They're all real fish that you can find in Australia!

BEAUTIFULLY
BIZARRE BIRDS

Dinosaurs may have gone extinct, but in a way they're alive and all around us. The two-legged group of dinosaurs known as therapods, which includes the *Tyrannosaurus rex* and the *Velociraptor*, are the ancestors of modern **birds.**

Over millions of years, descendants of these dinosaurs evolved in strange ways, developing feathers (yup, feathers are older than birds), losing their teeth, becoming warm-blooded, and shrinking in size. Over the years, these evolutionary changes continued as early birds adapted to survive in their environments. This is why penguins, for example, have waterproof feathers and are about 30 per cent blubber (fat) to stay warm in the cold Antarctic. Today, there are about 10,000 bird species around the world. Here are some of the most remarkable things about them ...

Not only do we know that birds sing in their dreams, but scientists have also worked out how to tell what they're dreaming about. When birds sing in their dreams, they move the muscles in their neck – by

watching these muscle movements, scientists can tell which birdsong they're singing (e.g. a male singing to attract a female).

Birds can't sweat. Instead, they use about 75 per cent of the air they inhale to act like an internal fan to cool down.

Birds can see the same colours we can, PLUS four extra ones: ultraviolet+red, ultraviolet+green, ultraviolet+yellow and ultraviolet+purple.

Bar-Tailed Godwits

The bar-tailed godwit is a long-billed, long-legged wading bird that holds the record for the furthest journey by a migrating bird. Every year, it flies about 7,500 miles from Alaska to New Zealand. The flight takes so much energy that by the time it arrives, it's lost half its body weight.

Bowerbirds

Male bowerbirds build large elaborate structures called bowers to show off to females, and decorate them with shiny and coloured objects to attract their attention. The females tour the different 'houses' to decide which male is the most impressive. Males will even steal shiny things from rivals. You can find these birds in Papua New Guinea and parts of Australia.

The female bowerbird can imitate the voices of different predators to scare away other birds if she feels threatened in her nest.

Chickens

Here's a weird fact about Australia's Sydney Opera House: the theatre has a net above the orchestra, which was installed in the 1980s when a real chicken wandered off stage during a performance and fell on top of a surprised cellist.

If you want chickens to lay the most eggs, play them pop music on the radio.

The *cock-a-doodle-doo* of roosters may seem incredibly loud to us, but roosters can't actually hear how loud their crowing is.

Chickens have a 'vocabulary' of over 200 different sounds to communicate with.

If you were a rich person in Denmark a thousand years ago, your family would bury you with a hen when you died. If you were really rich, you were buried with a goose. Both were considered holy.

Cormorants

In China, on the Lijiang River, fishermen use a traditional trick to catch lots of fish – they train cormorants to catch them for them. Cormorants are large black waterbirds that are expert divers, flapping their wings to dive as deep as 45 metres. There are records of the Chinese using them to

catch fish as far back as 2,600 years ago. The problem is, of course, that the cormorants want to eat the fish that they catch, so the fishermen keep them on a leash tied around their neck, which stops them from swallowing the catch.

Crows

Crows have been seen having fun teasing cats by pulling their tails. **Jackdaws** (a small type of black crow) will do it for a crafty reason: it pulls a cat's tail to distract it, so another jackdaw can steal the cat's food while its back is turned.

Did you know that crows can hold grudges? Scientists at the University of Washington found this out in an experiment. They divided their team into groups of two – half of the people wore scary face masks and the other half wore smiling face masks. The people wearing the scary face masks then

captured the crows in cages, before releasing them. When the scientists came back a few weeks later, the crows remembered their captors, and swooped down to attack only the people wearing the scary masks.

Crows and ravens are better than parrots at imitating the voices of humans.

Ducks

You probably know parrots can talk, but did you know that ducks can, too? We discovered this in the 1980s when an Australian musk duck named Ripper was recorded insulting his keeper, angrily calling him an idiot all day long.

Have you ever wondered if a duck's feet get cold in the water? They have a clever trick to deal with the colder winter temperatures – they stop the blood flow to the foot, which makes it numb and they can't feel it.

Ducks sleep with one eye open to watch for predators. Only half their brain sleeps while they do this. Then they close that eye and open the other one, and the other half of the brain will sleep.

Eagles

Bald eagles aren't actually bald – their name comes from the Old English word *balde*, which means 'white', for the white feathers on their head, neck and tail.

Bald eagles can use their wings to swim. They use a technique similar to the butterfly stroke of human swimmers.

One of the world's biggest eagles is the **harpy eagle**, which is mostly found in Central and South America. It's so large that its talons are bigger than a grizzly bear's claw. They've been seen swooping down with their 2-metre wingspan and snatching adult sloths out of trees.

In March 2023, keepers at the World Bird Sanctuary in Missouri, USA, noticed that their 31-year-old bald eagle named Murphy had built a nest and was protecting an egg. Murphy had decided he wanted to be a parent, but there was just one problem: his 'egg' was a rock. Murphy didn't realise

this, however, and he was so aggressive in protecting his 'egg' that he had to be moved to his own enclosure. Then the keepers heard of a baby eaglet that needed parents, and so they secretly swapped the rock with the eaglet without Murphy realising. Murphy began raising the adopted baby as his own.

Falcons

In Australia, **brown falcons** are also known as 'arson birds' ('arson' is the word for the crime of setting fire to things). This is because brown falcons have been seen picking up burning twigs from natural occurrences like forest fires and carrying the burning wood to other locations, to smoke out their prey. They've been using this trick a long time – it's thought falcons discovered the use of fire before humans did!

The gyrfalcon is the largest falcon in the world, and is found on the Arctic coasts and tundra. In 2009 scientists found an Arctic gyrfalcon nest in the Arctic which had been built over 2,500 years ago, and had been used by the birds ever since.

Flamingos

The last flamingo in Australia died in 2018. His name was Chile. Large flocks of flamingos used to roam the Australian outback, feeding on crustaceans near the pink Lake Eyre. But then the last ice age killed them all off, and the only flamingos Australia had were the ones brought from other countries to live in zoos. No more flamingoes will be brought to Australia, as the government is worried they might have diseases that could spread to other animals.

Flamingos are pink because they eat so much algae, brine fly larvae and brine shrimp, which are full of a red-orange pigment called beta-carotene.

Flamingo egg yolks can be slightly pink.

Geese

Geese sometimes fly upside down. They do this to drop down quickly when coming into land. At the

same time, they keep their head and neck the right way up. This manoeuvre is called 'whiffling'.

Bar-headed geese have been spotted flying over Mount Everest.

Hawks

When they want to get a better view, Harris's hawks will hop up onto their friends' shoulders. It's called 'back-stacking'.

Hoatzin

In the Amazon jungle, there's a tropical bird called the hoatzin, also known as the Canje pheasant, which has beautifully colourful feathers. It makes a different sound for each body movement it makes – for example, when it unfolds its wings it makes a croaky grunt, a bit like an old man getting out of a chair. When it calls to another hoatzin bird, it sounds like a crow with a cold.

The hoatzin is nicknamed the 'stink bird' for its distinctive smell. It absolutely reeks, because it digests leaves and plants just like a cow, so produces a powerful smell similar to manure, which helps keeps predators (and everything else) away.

Hummingbirds

The hummingbird is the only bird that can fly backwards. It can even fly upside down, as its wings can move in all directions, unlike most other birds.

Hummingbird eggs are the size of jelly beans.

Nightingales

A nightingale can sing for up to 20 seconds without taking a breath.

Ostriches

Ostriches have four kneecaps. (By the way, the tennis player Andy Murray has three.)

Ostriches don't ever need to drink – they absorb water from the plants they eat.

Owls

In 1996, in the British village of Stokeinteignhead, Devon, a man named Neil Simmons would go out into his garden at night to hoot at owls, until finally one evening an owl hooted back at him. The two had a hooting conversation every night for over a

year, until Mr Simmons discovered that the 'owl' was actually his neighbour, who also thought he had been having conversations with an owl.

Not all birds make their nests in trees. The **American burrowing owl** digs down into the ground to make a subterranean home, and lines the walls with cow dung to keep it warm.

Barn owls have one ear higher than the other. This helps them work out exactly where a noise is coming from.

Parrots

In 2018, a parrot was arrested in Brazil when it was discovered that it had been trained to alert its owners when the police were nearby, by shouting 'Mum, the police!'

Parrots give each other high-fives with their feet.

The Victorian scientist Francis Buckland would keep a parrot on a perch at home, overlooking the street. The parrot's favourite thing to do was to shout for taxis from the open window.

The New Zealand kākāpō bird, which is also called the owl parrot or moss chicken, is a parrot that lives on the ground and can grow up to 64 cm long. The world's heaviest parrot, it's also the only parrot that can't fly. The males have a wonderfully deep mating call, which is so loud that it can be heard from four miles away. The only problem is that females can't tell which direction it's coming from.

Among **kea parrots**, laughter is contagious – if one starts to laugh, they all get the giggles together.

In 2017, a man in Taiwan stole a parrot and then gave himself up to police because he couldn't take the endless squawking any longer.

African grey parrots have been known to have a vocabulary of 950 words, and live for as long as 75 years.

Wild parrots in New York City have built their nests on power lines and frequently cause power cuts.

Budgerigars grind their beaks when they're happy, like a cat purring.

Yawning budgies make other budgies yawn.

Partridges

A baby partridge is called a 'cheeper'.

The word 'partridge' comes from the ancient Greek word *pérdomai*, meaning 'farter', because of the noise the bird's wings make when it flies.

Penguins

Adélie penguins can swim as fast as 24.8 mph, and can leap out of the water as high as 3 metres, which is the closest they'll ever get to flying.

With emperor penguins, only the males produce milk for feeding their young. (With pigeons and flamingos, both males and females can make milk.) The loving dads have also been known to go 115 days without food in order to stay still and keep the eggs warm.

Emperor penguins can dive deeper than any other bird, and deeper than humans. Usually they reach depths of 100–200 metres, but the deepest emperor penguin dive recorded is 565 metres, spending 32.2 minutes under the water. This is more than double the deepest a human has ever dived using just one breath, which was 213.9 metres in 2007 by Herbert Nitsch.

Penguins can't pee, but they are powerful poopers – in 2003, Japanese scientists worked out that penguins can blast poop from their bottoms across a distance of 1.2 metres.

Phoenix Fowl

The **Japanese phoenix fowl** has the longest feather of any bird – their tail plumage can reach 10 metres in length, which means if they sat on top of a standard telephone pole their tail would almost touch the ground.

Pigeons

Pigeons find their way around when flying by following our roads and roundabouts.

Pitohuis

The **hooded pitohui**, found in New Guinea, is one of the world's only poisonous birds. The medium-sized songbird has toxins in its skin and in its reddish-brown and black feathers, which can kill predators, pests and even humans. Its name means 'rubbish bird', which the locals gave it once they realised they couldn't eat it. It's thought that the bird doesn't make the poison itself, but it gets it from eating a type of poisonous *Chorisine* beetle.

Puffins

A baby puffin is called a puffling. In Iceland, every year the people of the Westman Islands help baby pufflings get down to the sea by throwing them off cliffs.

You won't see a puffin drop food from its mouth. The roof of its mouth has sharp spines pointing back to its throat that stop fish from wriggling out.

Robins

Most people think that bulls hate the colour red, and will charge at you if you wave a red cloth at them. This isn't actually true, the colour red doesn't bother bulls at all. It does, however, bother robins, who think the flash of red is the sign of a rival, and will viciously attack.

Cave Swiftlets

This species of swift lives in caves on the Indonesian islands of Sumatra, Java and Bali. It builds its nest using its own spit as cement.

Shrikes

Shrikes are also known as butcherbirds, because of their gruesome way of killing their prey. Mostly found in Europe, Africa and North America, shrikes don't mess around when it comes to meal time – they'll snatch insects, rodents, and any other creature they can carry, and impale them on the nearest spikey branch or piece of barbed wire. If there's nothing sharp around, they'll trap them by wedging them into the crook of a tree branch.

Shrikes can imitate the voices of their prey to call out and lure them into their trap.

Sooty Terns

The sooty tern sleeps 'on the wing' – this means it sleeps while flying through the air over the sea! It does this in quick power naps of two to three seconds.

Tailorbirds

The tailorbird got its name from its habit of carefully making its nest by punching holes in leaves and using long blades of grass to sew them together.

Thrushes

The Australian Bassian thrush has a unique trick for finding food – it blasts the ground with its farts to blow the leaves away and reveal worms.

Turkeys

Male turkeys blush when they see female turkeys.

Turkeys keep cool by spraying their legs with their own poo.

Wild turkeys can run as fast as 25 mph, and fly as fast as 55 mph.

If you want to tell whether a turkey is male or female look at its poop – a male turkey poops a spiral shape, while a female tends to poop in the shape of the letter 'J'.

In Turkey, the word for a turkey translates as 'Indian bird'. In India, it's 'Peruvian bird'. In Greece, a turkey is a 'French bird'; and in Malaysia, it's a 'Dutch chicken'.

Vultures

London Zoo's first animal was a griffin vulture called Dr Brooks. He was soon joined by hundreds more creatures, including a marabou stork that at one point swallowed the cat that the zoo employed to catch rats. (With a bit of coaxing, the stork eventually spat the cat back out.)

Natural gas companies have used **turkey vultures** to detect leaks in pipes. The gas smells similar to rotting animals, which attracts the vultures.

Rüppell's vulture is the highest flying bird – it can cruise at over 11,300 metres, which is higher than most aeroplanes.

Female **Egyptian vultures** like males with the yellowest faces. If a male wants to make his face more yellow to attract her, he can do it in a rather disgusting way: he has to eat cow poop.

Turkey vultures cool down on a hot day by peeing on their own legs.

Weaver birds

Weaver birds build huge nests with lots of different rooms. As many as 400 weaver birds can live together in the same nest, which can be used continually for 100 years.

Woodpeckers

A woodpecker bangs its head against trees at 15 mph, 12,000 times a day.

Woodpeckers have shock-absorbing 'corrugated cartilage' to cushion their skulls from injury when they peck away like jackhammers at trees. Scientists are copying this woodpecker feature to make safer bike helmets.

A woodpecker's tongue is so long that it doesn't just go to the back of its mouth, it actually goes all the way around the back of its skull. It also has a spiky tip for skewering grubs.

Wren

Wrens are so small and light that if you gathered 1,400 together on a measuring scale, they would weigh the same as one swan.

WHO'S THE SMARTEST?

Bird Round

1. True or false? There's a rock band with a parrot as the lead singer.

It's **TRUE**. 'Hatebeak' is an American heavy-metal band featuring a parrot called Waldo as the singer. The band have made two albums – the second was made with the band Caninus, which has two dogs as its lead singers.

2. True or false? If a bald eagle loses a feather from one wing, it can't fly.

It's **FALSE**. In fact, when an eagle notices that it's dropped a feather from a wing, it immediately pulls out another feather from the opposite wing to keep itself perfectly balanced.

3. True or false? People used to believe that geese grew on trees.

It's **TRUE**. People in medieval Europe didn't know how geese produced offspring, because they flew north to nest and had their young where no one could see them. So people thought the geese must grow like fruit on special trees.

4. True or false? There are venomous birds.

It's **FALSE**. No birds are known to bite or inject you with venom, BUT there are toxic birds like the pitohui and the ifrita of Papua New Guinea, and the bronzewing pigeon of Australia, which absorb poison from animals and plants they eat and become poisonous to eat, and are even dangerous to touch.

5. True or false? The tufted puffin can hold 10 fish in its mouth at once.

It's **FALSE**. The largest of all puffin species, the tufted puffin can hold even more! It can cram 20 fish in its mouth to bring to its chicks.

6. True or false? The African marabou stork eats rubbish.

It's **TRUE**. These bizarre birds, which can grow to 1.5 metres tall with a wing-span of 3.6 metres, will eat just about anything, including other birds. But they especially like to visit rubbish tips and have been seen snacking on junk like shoes and metal.

7. True or false? The golden pheasant is a rainbow-coloured gamebird found only in the mountains of China.

It's **FALSE** – you can also find the golden pheasant in other countries around the world including Canada, Colombia, Australia and Hawaii, and even Norfolk, UK!

8. True or false? The 'magnificent frigatebird' steals other birds' food before they can eat it.

It's **FALSE** – the magnificent frigatebird steals the food after another bird eats it. It forces its victim to throw up, and the frigatebird then feeds on the upchucked mess.

9. True or false? The rufous potoo is an Amazonian bird that doesn't build a nest but lays a single egg on top of a tall tree stub.

It's **TRUE**. It's the only bird that does this. Laying its egg like this means predators can't get to it.

10. True or false? The kagu flaps its wings to scare away predators.

It's **FALSE** – this flightless bird selflessly flaps its wings to make itself look injured, to lure a predator away from its chicks.

RIDICULOUSLY
RIVETING
REPTILES

For over 150 million years, **reptiles** ruled the Earth in their dinosaur form. Modern reptiles no longer have the sheer size of those mega creatures, but that doesn't mean they're any less scary, or any less varied. Reptiles are cold-blooded (but are able to warm themselves up by basking in the sun), have scaly skin, and lay leathery eggs that they can leave far away in water. There are four basic types of reptiles: crocodiles and alligators, turtles and tortoises, snakes and lizards. Let's start with the toothiest ...

Alligators

You can tell the difference between an alligator and a crocodile by looking at them when their jaws are closed. If you can see teeth on the outside of the upper jaw, it's an alligator – if you can see teeth outside the lower jaw as well, it's a crocodile.

Whether it's a male or female baby alligator that will hatch from an egg is down to how warm their nest is. If the eggs sit in a nest at 30 degrees Fahrenheit the offspring will be female, but if it's a bit warmer at 34 degrees, they'll be male.

Alligators can go up to three years without food.

Alligators have about 75 teeth in their mouth at any given time, however they constantly fall out from use and are replaced with new ones. Over its lifetime, the alligator will probably get through about 3,000 teeth.

Despite their bloodthirsty reputation, alligators have also been found to enjoy meals of fruit and vegetables. They even help these plants to spread by pooping out their seeds.

If alligators and crocodiles are in a lake that starts to freeze, they poke their snouts up out of the water like a snorkel to breathe, and let the lake freeze solid around them. They then go into a kind of hibernation called 'brumation' until it thaws.

Alligators are tough as nails. In 2019, a large lorry was driving down a highway in Florida, USA, when it collided head-on at full speed with a huge alligator that was 3.7 metres long and weighing 210 kg. The alligator was dizzy for a second, but was fine and walked away. The lorry was damaged!

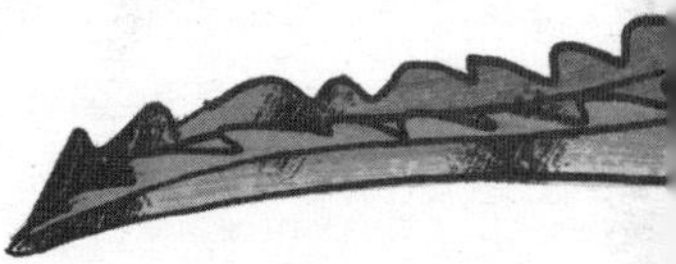

Alligators can move up to 35 mph across short distances on land. For comparison, Olympic gold medallist Usain Bolt has a top speed of about 28 mph.

Crocodiles

The word 'crocodile' comes from the ancient Greek name for the creature, *krokodilos*, which means 'worm of the stones'.

Most kinds of crocodile carry their young in their mouths, but the gharial crocodile of India has

a long snout that is too narrow for this. So the babies have to hitch a ride on its head and back. Gharial dads can have babies with as many as eight different mothers, which means they can end up carrying over 100 young ones on their head and shoulders as they swim around.

Gharial and **mugger crocodiles** in the Himalayan foothills have been turning bright orange. While they look like they've been spraying themselves with fake tan, it turns out that the water the crocodiles like to lie in is full of iron oxide (rust), which slowly stains their skin orange.

The ancient Greeks and Egyptians made their lipstick from crocodile poop.

While today you only find **Nile crocodiles** in Africa, in 2023 paleontologists found evidence that 4.5 million years ago there were crocodiles that were very similar living in southern Spain.

The largest crocodile in captivity is 120 years old and named Cassius. When he was last measured in 2011, Cassius was a colossal 5.48 metres long, which is about two thirds the length of a London bus. His keepers at Marineland Crocodile Park in Australia think he's probably grown even bigger since then, but haven't dared try to remeasure him.

In 2023, scientists announced the first ever recorded case of a female crocodile producing eggs without needing the involvement of a male. We knew that birds, sharks, lizards and snakes could do this, but now we know crocodiles can have a 'virgin birth' too.

As recently as 1,300 years ago, there were CROCODILES WITH HORNS living on the island of Madagascar.

120 million years ago, in what is now South Korea, there were 3-metre-long crocodiles that walked on two hind legs.

Geckos

Geckos have vision 350 times more powerful than ours!

At 14–18 mm in length, the **Jaragua dwarf gecko** is smaller than some ant species.

Geckos don't have eyelids, but a transparent membrane (like a skin) that protects their eyes. If they get something stuck in their eye, they can simply lick it off.

The **Asian tokay gecko** is named after the sound of its call – while some people hear it shouting 'tokay', other people have sworn they heard it shout 'gecko'.

Even though they're probably best known for their wall-climbing ability, half of all gecko species can't climb walls.

When they're attacked by predators, geckos can shed their tail, which flops around by itself to distract the attacker while the gecko runs away. The tail will grow back, but shorter than it was before.

Geckos have millions of tiny hairs called setae that hook into solid surfaces. The sucking force of all these hairs is theoretically strong enough to hold up two adult humans.

When geckos cross a wet surface, the thousands of tiny hairs on their feet trap air bubbles underneath them, which the geckos then walk on. So really, they're hovering!

If the giant leaf-tailed gecko feels threatened, it throws its jaws wide open to flash its bright red mouth as a warning, and then lets out a piercing scream that sounds just like the cry of a human child.

Ichthyosaur

The largest meat-eating reptile to ever live roamed the oceans millions of years ago – the Ichthyosaur grew up to 21.3 metres long - that's the length of seven buses!

Iguana

The Galapagos marine iguana is one of only two animals that can live entirely off seaweed as its only food. The other animal? A sheep! Specifically the North Ronaldsay sheep, which lives on the Orkney Islands.

Komodo Dragons

The largest lizards on Earth, the Indonesian **Komodo dragon**, can grow up to three metres long.

You wouldn't think a lizard so big could get even more dangerous, but the Komodo dragon has a deadly venomous bite just like a snake. And they will eat ANYTHING, whether it's water buffalo, humans or each other!

Baby Komodo dragons roll around in poo and live up in the trees so that adult Komodo dragons can't eat them.

Lizards

The Gila monster is a species of venomous lizard found in southern USA and Mexico. It has a magnificent forked tongue that serves a purpose. The Gila monster uses it to 'taste' smells in 3D, like radar, letting it work out exactly where the source of the smell is.

The **blue-tongued skink lizard** of Australia and Papua New Guinea defends itself by puffing itself up and waggling its unusually blue tongue at enemies while hissing.

The armadillo girdled lizard of South Africa has the rare ability to defend itself from predators by curling up into a ball and holding this pose by biting down on the tip of its tail. Its thick scales then protect it from attack.

The **Texas horned lizard** defends itself from predators with a pretty strange weapon: it **SQUIRTS BLOOD** from its **EYES**. It can hit targets 1.5 metres away.

Several species of lizard on the island of New Guinea have blood, bones, muscles, tongues and flesh that are all bright green. This is because of the unusually high amounts of green pigment in their bile (body fluids), which overpowers the crimson colour of their red blood cells.

Side-blotched lizards, which are commonly found in the deserts of western North America, have three rankings of males that you can identify from their bright throat colour. Males with orange throats are highly aggressive; males with yellow-striped throats are called 'sneakers' and are more cowardly; and

blue-throated lizards can fight off the yellows but not the oranges.

The thorny devil lizard drinks through its skin.

The **chameleon's** tongue is twice as long as its body.

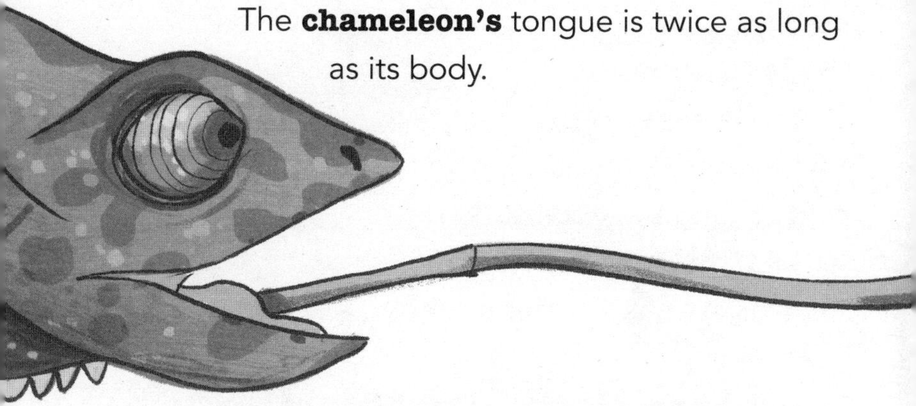

The plumed basilisk can scamper across water at a speed of about 4.8 miles per hour, using the air pockets under its webbed feet to push off the water. This is why it's nicknamed the 'Jesus Christ lizard'.

The **earless monitor lizard** is incredibly rare. It spends its days hidden in tunnels under riverbeds, coming out at night to feed. It has a few tricks to help with this: its eyelids are see-through, for example, so it can still see even when its eyes are closed. And in order to prevent being swept away by the river, it finds a large stone and wraps its tail around it to use like an anchor.

There's a lizard that lives in Ecuador's Cloud Forest that has a snout so long (about one third of its body length) that it's known as the Pinocchio lizard. It's thought that it uses this extra-long nose to look more impressive to females. The Pinocchio lizard also turns white when it sleeps.

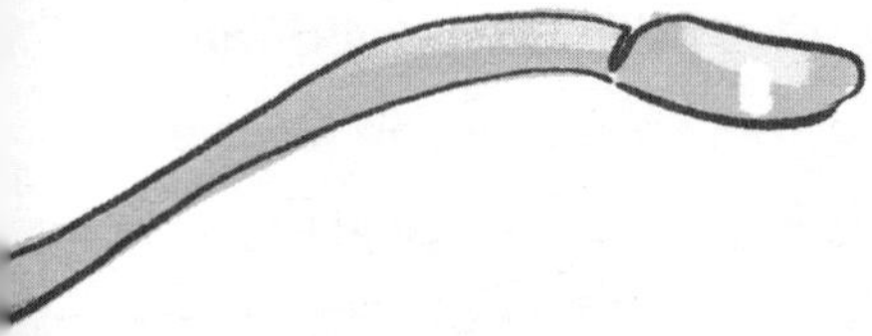

The Australian **perentie lizard** is one of the fastest lizards in the world. It can run as fast as an Olympic sprinter.

There are lizards known as legless lizards that look just like snakes. In the UK, one such species is the slow worm. You can tell them apart from snakes by the fact that they have eyelids and external ear openings, don't have broad belly scales, have a notched not a forked tongue, and have a very long tail (snakes have a long body and short tail).

SSsnakesss

The largest snake that ever existed is the ***Titanoboa***, which lived about 60 million years ago in the South American jungles. It was over 15 metres long, about the same as three and a half Volkswagen Beetle cars. We only discovered its remains in 2009.

Alice Roosevelt, the daughter of the US president Theodore Roosevelt, kept a pet snake in the White House and called it Emily Spinach. Other presidents' pets that have lived in America's most important building include grizzly bears, silkworms, alligators, tigers, a guinea pig called Fighting Bob Evans, a hen called Baron Spreckle, a black bear called Jonathan Edwards, a laughing hyena called Bill, a parrot called Polly who swore A LOT and a pygmy hippo called William Johnson Hippopotamus.

Rattlesnakes are named for the rattle at the end of their tail. It's made of keratin, the same stuff that your hair and nails are made of. Their rattles get longer over their lifetime – every time a rattlesnake sheds its skin, it adds another segment to its rattle.

Pythons and boa constrictors have tiny hind leg bones that they can't use. This is because their ancestor that lived millions of years ago had legs.

The smallest known snake is the **Barbados threadsnake**, which wins the Most Adorable award for being about the same size as half a stalk of spaghetti.

A male red-sided garter snake has a lot of competition when it comes to attracting a female (males can 'tail-wrestle' with each other to fight for a female they like), but some have a trick. They can release a pheromone scent that makes the other males think it's female. While his competition is distracted by him, he can swoop in on the females.

Ilha da Queimada Grande is an island off the coast of Brazil, more commonly known as Snake Island. At only 106 acres (less than a third of the size of London's Hyde Park), it's pretty tiny but at one count, it was thought to be home to about 430,000 snakes.

Dice snakes escape predators by playing dead – but they do it by putting on a really convincing show. If they see an attacker coming they poop, bleed from their mouths, and flop onto their backs, all to make themselves look too dead and disgusting to eat.

Tortoises

Desert tortoises worry about dehydration a lot. This is why they dig basins to catch rain, and always go back to check on them every time there's a storm.

The names of real tortoise species include the pancake tortoise, the geometric tortoise, the impressed tortoise and the Wolf Volcano giant tortoise.

The ancient Greek philosopher Aeschylus was accidentally killed when an eagle dropped a tortoise on his head.

The first animals to ever go to deep space were two Horsfield's tortoises sent by the Soviet Space Program to travel around the Moon in 1968. The tortoises made it back to Earth alive, having travelled faster than any animal in history.

Tuatara

This New Zealand lizard-like reptile has a third eye! You can only see it on the young hatchlings, before it gets covered up by its scales. The eye is sensitive to light, so it's thought it helps the tuatara figure out what time of day it is.

The tuatara is the only living member of the order *Rhynchocephalia*, a group of animals that goes back 200 million years and went extinct 60 million years ago.

The tuatara has a unique set of teeth – they're arranged with two rows in the upper jaw that close around a single row on the bottom jaw. And they're not technically teeth, but parts of the jaw bone. This means if one snaps off it won't grow a replacement.

A male tuatara named Henry at the Southland Museum and Art Gallery in New Zealand became a father for the first time at the age of 111. He had 11 babies with a female named Mildred, who was in her seventies.

Turtles

The upper shell of turtles and tortoises is actually their ribcage. The underside of the shell is a different piece grown from the shoulder girdle and sternum (breastbone). So to say that turtles 'live inside' their shells is like saying you live inside your ribcage.

Turtles breathe through their bottoms.

The **alligator snapping turtle** tricks fish into swimming into its mouth. It uses its pink tongue like a fishing lure, lying still in water with its mouth open, wiggling the tongue. When a fish approaches the tongue thinking it's a worm – CHOMP – the turtle snaps its jaws shut.

The Chinese soft-shell turtle pees out of its mouth.

The **Australian white-throated snapping turtle** is also called the 'bum-breathing turtle', as it can inhale nearly 70 per cent of all the oxygen it needs through its cloacal bursae – otherwise known as its butt.

No turtles have teeth.

The **Mary River turtle** has got to be the most stylish reptile of all – the Australian creature has a bright green mohawk haircut, with a wispy green goatee on its chin. This isn't actually hair, but algae growing on its skin. It's incredibly rare – in 2017, it was estimated that only 136 of these punk-rocker turtles still existed in the wild.

The Madagascar big-headed turtle has – surprise! – an unusually big head, but this isn't actually its weirdest feature. While its head has a fantastic rainbow colour, the critically endangered turtle has a shell so brilliantly yellow that it looks like it's wearing a suit of shiny gold armour.

WHO'S THE SMARTEST?

Reptile Round

1. True or false? There's a snake that can fly.

It's **FALSE** … but **ALMOST TRUE**. There is a type of snake known as the flying snake, but it doesn't fly, it glides. First, it climbs up trees by pushing its ridged scales against the rough tree bark, and then it jumps from the tree, flattening its body like a wing. It can glide to another tree 100 metres away, or down to the ground to pounce on its prey.

2. True or false? You can keep a tortoise in the fridge.

It's **TRUE**, as long as it's just for winter. Putting a tortoise in a refrigerator during the 6–12 weeks of winter when they hibernate can actually be good for its health, as long as you occasionally open the door to give it fresh air.

3. True or false? You can buy rattlesnake perfume.

It's **FALSE** – you can't buy it, but ground squirrels in America make their own rattlesnake perfume and wear it to keep the snakes away. The squirrels chew on old rattlesnake skins and then wipe the chewed skin all over their fur.

4. True or false? The frilled lizard of northern Australia and New Guinea has a large frill around its neck that it opens to use as a sail while swimming.

It's **FALSE**. It does have a huge orange frilled collar that unfolds like a sail, but it uses it as a scary display to frighten away predators and to attract females.

5. True or false? The mata mata is a turtle with a head that looks exactly like a leaf.

It's **TRUE.** The South American freshwater turtle has a rough brown shell that looks like tree bark, and head like a leaf, that serves as excellent camouflage.

6. True or false? The Malagasy leaf-nosed snake has a snout that looks exactly like a leaf.

It's **TRUE**. Found on Madagascar, the snake with the strangely long green snout uses the feature as camouflage, luring prey towards the 'leaf' before it suddenly strikes.

7. True or false? The pig-nosed turtle has a snout so big that it can't swim underwater.

It's **FALSE**. In fact, its piggy nose acts like a snorkel, helping it to swim even better in the waters off the Australian coast.

8. True or false? The boomslang snake is named after the farting noise it makes when it eats.

It's **FALSE**. *Boomslang* means 'tree snake' in Dutch and Afrikaans. It's highly venomous and looks exactly like a tree branch, so if you're ever walking around in sub-Saharan Africa be careful when grabbing a tree.

9. True or false? The Moorish gecko can change colour to match its environment, even when it can't see what colour that is.

It's **TRUE**. The Moorish gecko has sensors in its skin that 'see' the levels of light and let it know what shade to change colour to. Scientists tested this by blindfolding the reptile.

10. True or false? The yacare caiman attracts a mate by performing a water dance.

It's **TRUE**. The small South American member of the crocodile family lets out a low rumbling call underwater, and then performs a dance routine to impress females.

ASTOUNDINGLY
AWESOME
AMPHIBIANS

400 million years ago, before reptiles, mammals and birds, the **amphibians** ruled the world. This group of animals are semi-aquatic – they need to live close to lakes, rivers and coastlines to keep their skin moist and to lay their eggs away from land predators. Some of the rarest and most endangered animals on Earth are amphibians. This group is made up of frogs and toads, salamanders, and 'caecilians' (pronounced sir-silly-anns, which sounds really close to Sicilian but definitely should not be confused with a person from Sicily). Maybe we should start with these first ...

Caecilians

Caecilians are a group of long amphibians without arms or legs often confused for worms or snakes. In fact, they are their own group of amphibian. They live mostly secret lives, hiding in the ground or in riverbeds in South and Central America, Africa and southern Asia, living off grubs and earthworms which they snatch with their wide open mouths.

There are more than 220 species of caecilians known to science, and their size differences are pretty wild. The shortest known caecilian is the 8.9 cm-long Makumunu Assumbo in Cameroon, while the

largest is a 1.5 metre-long monster with the very proper name of Thompson's caecilian, which you can find in Colombia.

Caecilians usually have very small eyes (while some don't have eyes at all), and they can only see differences in light and dark. In some caecilian species the eyes are under their skin, which protects them while they live underground.

Caecilian skin is smooth and slippery like soap. As well as being slippery they've got other defences as well – some species, like Boettger's caecilian in South America, have toxins in their skin that scare away predators. (So probably not a good idea to try and grab it after all.)

The cloud forests of Ecuador, on the slopes of the Andean mountains, are the home of the giant caecilian ***Caecilia pachynema***, which is 90 cm long.

Humans don't have much to fear from caecilians as they're not dangerous to us – which is fortunate,

because when you see their teeth it DEFINITELY seems like they could be dangerous if they wanted to. They have mouths full of glinting razor-sharp teeth that look like rows of needles.

Adult caecilians also have an unusual way of feeding their young. They don't feed them milk like mammals do, and they don't feed them chewed-up food like bird parents. Instead, the mother caecilian lets their children scrape off a layer of her **SKIN** to eat, which is frankly too disgusting to think about.

Frogs

More than 4,000 species of frog can flick their tongues out and grab insects faster than the human eye can see. Partly this is because their tongues are attached at their lower jaw, not the back of the throat like our human tongues. (Just imagine how useful an extendable tongue would be for eating cinema popcorn straight from the bucket.)

The **yellow-blotched glassfrog** from Ecuador is the most transparent of all amphibians – if you look at it from below, you can see its heart, lungs, intestines, bones and veins through skin as clear as crystal.

Wallace's flying frog is a Southeast Asian frog that leaps off high tree branches and uses its webbed feet to glide across to the next tree.

Frog tongues can be strong, too. The **horned frog** can use its tongue to pull objects 1.4 times heavier than its own body weight.

The bright green red-eyed tree frog uses colour very cleverly. Its green body colour means it blends into the surrounding leaves of the Central American jungles. But if a predator spots it, it pops its eyelids open to show its bright red eyes as a warning. It then flashes its orange feet, and the blue stripes of its thighs, all of which startle the attacker. As the predator hesitates, the frog leaps away.

There is a tiny frog called the **pinkletink**. It lives in Martha's Vineyard, USA.

In India, there's a frog that's purple – it's called the purple frog; or sometimes the pignose frog. We only discovered it in 2003 because it likes to spend nearly all of its time buried 8 metres underground, eating termites.

The tongue of a frog is ten times softer than your tongue.

There are two particularly weird things about the Brazilian pumpkin toadlet. One is that scientists discovered they glow in the dark under ultraviolet light, as they have fluorescent skeletons. The other curious thing is its call. When the frog calls out to its friends, it does so with a sound that is actually too low for any other pumpkin toadlets to hear. Unfortunately, predators can hear it ...

The **Titicaca water frog** is a large creature that was once voted the second-ugliest animal in the world, below the blobfish. It's only found in the South American region of Lake Titicaca, high above sea level on the border of Bolivia and Peru. The frog used to be a common sight in the area but it has become endangered, mainly because local people capture it for food to sell to tourists. It's also believed that you can make medicine by blending the frog into a smoothie, but there isn't actually any evidence that this works.

While the most famous venomous animals are snakes, there are some seriously deadly frogs

too. Some frogs are poisonous if eaten, but the most deadly are the ones that can inject venom. Just 1 g of poison from the Bruno's casque-headed frog, for example, is enough to KILL 80 people, or 30,000 mice. This works out to being 25 times more poisonous than the bite of a Brazilian pit-viper. The frog doesn't bite, but uses spiky spines sticking out of its head to inject poison into anything that grabs it.

Some frogs let out an ear-splittingly loud scream, but it's so high-pitched that humans can't hear it. Scientists in the Amazon noticed small **leaf litter frogs** throwing back their head and opening their mouths wide, but apparently making no noise. They recorded the frogs anyway, and when they played it back they realised that they'd captured the first example of 'defensive ultrasound' by amphibians. It's thought they do this to summon other animals to attack a predator threatening them.

Alaska's wood frog has a clever trick to survive icy temperatures – it floods its blood with glucose (sugar) which acts like antifreeze, and stops the frog freezing solid.

The **Cuyaba dwarf frog** inflates its bottom like a balloon to frighten away attackers.

The Malagasy rainbow frog is one of the most colourful creatures on the island of Madagascar, which is really saying something. When it's threatened, the frog will puff itself up to appear much larger, and then CHARGE at its attacker! It can also climb straight up vertical rock surfaces.

In the Sierra Nevada mountains of south-eastern Spain, you can find the **Betic midwife toad**, which is grey and mottled with dark specks and grows to about 3.5 cm long. The toad is so named because the male toad looks after the young. He carries the fertilised eggs on his hind legs until it's safe to let them go, at which point he drops them into lakes and ponds to hatch.

The Gardiner's Seychelles frog is probably the world's smallest frog. The adults only grow to a length of 11 mm, the same size as a drawing pin.

The Central African **hairy frog** is also known as the horror frog or Wolverine frog. Why these scary nicknames? Because of its bizarre behaviour when it feels like it's about to be attacked. To defend itself the hairy frog will **SNAP ITS OWN TOES** to turn them into sharp claws that poke out of its toe pads on its hind feet, for it to use as weapons.

The South African black rain frog is a fantastically grumpy-looking frog that looks a lot like an avocado. Perhaps its grumpiness is partly down to the fact that, unlike other frogs, it can't jump or swim. This makes escaping predators tricky, so it has developed a survival tactic of inflating its body with air to seven times its natural size to look scarier to pigs, birds and snakes looking to gobble it up. If this doesn't work, it can quickly dig a tunnel 20 cm deep to hide in.

The **motorbike frog** lives in Australia and is easy to identify – its loud call sounds exactly like a revving motorbike.

Scientists have found that male green tree frogs are so desperate for female attention that they answer to the sound of popcorn popping, a washing machine spinning, a dog drinking water, cannon firing in a civil war movie and ragtime music, thinking that these are all the sounds of a female's mating call.

The **Vietnamese mossy frog** is semi-aquatic, meaning it spends a large amount of its time in water, with only its eyes poking out, camouflaged by a skin that looks like green moss. As well as this survival trick, it can also throw its voice like a ventriloquist to trick predators into thinking that it's about 4 metres away from where it actually is.

Salamanders

When the North American **tiger salamander** eats its prey, it retracts (pulls back) its eyeballs into its head to press against the roof of its mouth. This pressure helps to force the food down its throat.

The Chinese giant salamander is the world's largest amphibian, growing to a length of 1.8 metres.

The largest *ever* amphibian, though, was much bigger. The Prionosuchus roamed the region now called Brazil about 280 million years ago. The largest specimen we've found is 5.5 metres long.

The **olm** is a cave-dwelling salamander that's completely blind. Unlike other salamanders, it's totally aquatic – it eats, sleeps and spends all of its time underwater. This is why the olm has transparent skin (it doesn't need pigment to block light). It uses its other super-developed senses of smell and hearing to hunt in the dark, but if it doesn't catch anything, it's not a problem. The olm can survive without food for 10 years.

The hellbender is North America's largest amphibian. Its scary name comes from its monster-like appearance. Its other not-very-flattering nicknames include the snot otter, lasagna lizard, devil dog, mud-devil, mud dog, water dog, grampus, Allegheny alligator and leverian water newt.

Even though the hellbender salamander has lungs, it has an unusual trick – it can absorb oxygen in water through its skin.

Lungless salamanders, like the Mexican climbing salamander, are a family of salamander with two unusual characteristics. As their name suggests, they aren't born with lungs, instead breathing through their skin and mouth lining. The other is that they don't have a larval stage – when they hatch, they are fully-formed, miniature adults ready to shoot their projectile tongue at insects. (To understand just how weird this is, it would be like humans not having a baby or child stage, instead being born as tiny adults able to walk and talk.)

Axolotls can regrow body parts they lose – not just tails, but also limbs, as well as parts of their brain, heart and lower jaw.

The giant palm salamander can stick its tongue in and out of its mouth 50 times in the same time it takes you to blink once.

In America, there is the **northern slimy salamander** (*Plethodon glutinosus*), which is covered in slime so sticky that when a snake or other predator bites it, the slime glues the attacker's mouth shut...

... which seems like the right fact to end this book on. I hope all of this has given you plenty of interesting, and occasionally disgusting, things to think about. Our world is such a strange, funny, exciting place, filled with amazing things. There's so much to see! Just think how boring life would be without animals to share it with. So, what are you waiting for? Get out into the world and start looking for some weird creatures!

WHO'S THE SMARTEST?

Amphibian Round

1. True or false? There was once a frog species that ate dinosaurs.

It's **TRUE**. Its name is Beelzebufo and it lived about 66-70 million years ago. We think it was a predator that ate young dinosaurs, and had a bite that was twice as powerful as a human's bite.

2. True or false? There's only one lizard species that can swim.

It's **TRUE**. The marine Galapagos lizard swims out to find food – not fish, but algae that it scrapes off rocks with its claws.

3. True or false? There's only one amphibian that has tentacles.

It's **TRUE**. Caecilians are the only amphibians with tentacles. They have them between their eyes and nostrils, and use them to explore their environment.

4. True or false? There's an English frog with a Norfolk accent.

It's **TRUE**. The northern pool frog is found in different places in Europe, but scientists discovered that the northern pool frogs that live in Norfolk have their own distinctive croak that they use as a mating call.

5. True or false? The Madagascan tomato frog is yellow.

It's **FALSE**. The tomato frog is red, of course. You didn't think I'd try to trick you, did you?

6. True or false? The Mexican bearded lizard only needs to eat once a month.

It's **FALSE**. It actually only needs to eat three meals a year!

7. True or false? The southern African grey foam-nest tree frog makes its nest out of foam made by ocean waves.

It's **FALSE**. The female grey foam-nest tree frog makes its own foam for a nest by oozing a secretion from its skin, and then whipping it up like meringue mix by kicking its legs. It then lays its eggs, and when the tadpoles hatch they fall through the foam into the pond or lake below.

8. True or false? Toads have to blink to swallow food.

It's **TRUE**. The blinking means they press their eyes into their mouths, and squeeze the food down their throats.

9. True or false? The longest salamander tongues are five times as long as the salamander's body.

It's **FALSE**. Some salamanders' tongues can be as much as ten times as long as their body.

10. True or false? When the blue-tongued skink lizard is attacked, it defends itself by sticking its tongue out.

It's **TRUE**. The lizard waits till the right moment, then tries to scare away the predator by doing the rudest thing it can think of – sticking out its tongue!

WEIRDEST FACTS TO TELL PEOPLE

WEIRDEST THINGS I LEARNED TODAY

MY TOP TEN WEIRDEST ANIMALS

1.

2.

3.

4.

5.

6.

7.

8.

9.

10.

ABOUT THE AUTHOR

Edward is a treasure hunter – not for gold (although he'd be very happy to find some!) but for strange and amazing facts and stories. He grew up surrounded by old maps and mysterious books, and now he writes incredible tales about forgotten sports, imaginary places, and of course, as you now know, the weird and wonderful world of animals and nature.

He belongs to the Royal Geographical Society, a club for map-lovers and explorers, and for many years dreamt up clever and intriguing questions for the TV show *QI*.

When he's not writing, Edward is at home in England, surrounded by maps and curiosities, and he is always looking for the next big mystery to share with curious minds like yours!

ABOUT THE ILLUSTRATOR

Jez Tuya lives and works in windy Wellington, New Zealand. When he was little, he wanted to fly aeroplanes—but he loved drawing even more so now he spends his days creating amazing pictures for children's books.

Jez has worked with lots of publishers all over the world and has even helped design characters for movies. Jez is married to Jane, and has three children called Orla, Ethan and Clara. When he's not drawing, he likes to cook delicious food, build model aeroplanes and spend time with his family.

UNTIL NEXT TIME ...

BV - #0001 - 300522 - C0 - 212/135/3 - PB - 9600690000192 - Gloss Lamination